Cambridge English: Preliminary 7

WITH ANSWERS

Official examination papers from University of Cambridge ESOL Examinations

CAMBRIDGE
UNIVERSITY PRESS

CAMBRIDGE UNIVERSITY PRESS
Cambridge, New York, Melbourne, Madrid, Cape Town,
Singapore, São Paulo, Delhi, Tokyo, Mexico City

Cambridge University Press
The Edinburgh Building, Cambridge CB2 8RU, UK

www.cambridge.org
Information on this title: www.cambridge.org/9781107675193

© Cambridge University Press 2012

It is normally necessary for written permission for copying to be obtained *in advance* from a publisher. The candidate answer sheets at the back of this book are designed to be copied and distributed in class. The normal requirements are waived here and it is not necessary to write to Cambridge University Press for permission for an individual teacher to make copies for use within his or her own classroom. Only those pages which carry the wording '© UCLES 2012 Photocopiable' may be copied.

First published 2012

Printed in the United Kingdom at the University Press, Cambridge

A catalogue record for this publication is available from the British Library

ISBN 978-1-107-675193   Student's Book with answers
ISBN 978-1-107-635661   Student's Book without answers
ISBN 978-1-107-638884   Audio CD Set
ISBN 978-1-107-610484   Self-study Pack

Cambridge University Press has no responsibility for the persistence or accuracy of URLs for external or third-party internet websites referred to in this publication, and does not guarantee that any content on such websites is, or will remain, accurate or appropriate. Information regarding prices, travel timetables and other factual information given in this work are correct at the time of first printing, but Cambridge University Press does not guarantee the accuracy of such information thereafter.

Contents

A Guide to Cambridge English: Preliminary 4

Test 1 14

Test 2 34

Test 3 54

Test 4 74

Frames for the Speaking test 94

Test 1 Key 106

Test 2 Key 121

Test 3 Key 136

Test 4 Key 151

Sample answer sheets 166

Acknowledgements 171

Visual material for the Speaking test colour section at centre of book

A Guide to Cambridge English: Preliminary

Cambridge English: Preliminary, also known as the *Preliminary English Test (PET)*, is part of a comprehensive range of exams developed by University of Cambridge ESOL Examinations (Cambridge ESOL). Cambridge English exams have similar characteristics, but are designed for different purposes and different levels of English language ability. *Cambridge English: Preliminary* is at Level B1 (*Threshold*) of the Council of Europe's Common European Framework of Reference for Languages (CEFR). It has also been accredited in the UK as an Entry Level 3 ESOL certificate in the UK's National Qualifications Framework.

Examination	Council of Europe Framework Level	UK National Qualifications Framework Level
Cambridge English: Proficiency *Certificate of Proficiency in English (CPE)*	C2	3
Cambridge English: Advanced *Certificate in Advanced English (CAE)*	C1	2
Cambridge English: First *First Certificate in English (FCE)*	B2	1
Cambridge English: Preliminary *Preliminary English Test (PET)*	B1	Entry 3
Cambridge English: Key *Key English Test (KET)*	A2	Entry 2

Cambridge English: Preliminary is accepted by employers, and further education and government departments for business, study and immigration purposes. It is also useful preparation for higher level exams, such as *Cambridge English: First*, *Cambridge English: Advanced* and *Cambridge English: Proficiency*.

Cambridge English: Preliminary is ideal for learners who need to use English in a practical everyday way to communicate, e.g. read simple textbooks and articles, write simple personal letters, and deal with most of the situations you might meet when travelling in an English-speaking country.

Cambridge English: Preliminary is also available in a version with exam content and topics specifically targeted at the interests and experience of school-aged learners. *Cambridge English: Preliminary for Schools,* also known as *Preliminary English Test (PET) for Schools*), follows exactly the same format and level, and leads to the same certificate as *Cambridge English: Preliminary.*

Topics

These are the topics used in the *Cambridge English: Preliminary* exam:

Clothes	Hobbies and leisure	Relations with other people
Daily life	House and home	Services
Education	Language	Shopping
Entertainment and media	Natural world	Social interaction
Environment	People	Sport
Food and drink	Personal feelings, opinions and experiences	Transport
Free time		Travel and holidays
Health, medicine and exercise	Personal identification	Weather
	Places and buildings	Work and jobs

Cambridge English: Preliminary content – an overview

Paper	Name	Timing	Content	Test focus
Paper 1	Reading/Writing	1 hour 30 minutes	Reading: Five parts which test a range of reading skills with a variety of texts, ranging from very short notices to longer continuous texts. Writing: Three parts which test a range of writing skills.	Assessment of candidates' ability to understand the meaning of written English at word, phrase, sentence, paragraph and whole text level. Assessment of candidates' ability to produce straightforward written English, ranging from producing variations on simple sentences to pieces of continuous text.
Paper 2	Listening	35 minutes (plus 6 minutes transfer time)	Four parts ranging from short exchanges to longer dialogues and monologues.	Assessment of candidates' ability to understand dialogues and monologues in both informal and neutral settings on a range of everyday topics.
Paper 3	Speaking	10–12 minutes per pair of candidates	Four parts: In Part 1, candidates interact with an examiner; In Parts 2 and 4, they interact with another candidate; In Part 3, they have an extended individual long turn.	Assessment of candidates' ability to express themselves in order to carry out functions at *Threshold* level. To ask and to understand questions and make appropriate responses. To talk freely on matters of personal interest.

Paper 1: Reading and Writing

Paper format
The Reading component contains five parts. The Writing component contains three parts.

Number of questions
Reading has 35 questions; Writing has seven questions.

Sources
Authentic and adapted-authentic real world notices; newspapers and magazines; simplified encyclopaedias; brochures and leaflets; websites.

A Guide to Cambridge English: Preliminary

Answering

Candidates indicate answers by shading lozenges (Reading), or writing answers (Writing) on an answer sheet.

Timing

1 hour 30 minutes.

Marks

Reading: Each of the 35 questions carries one mark. This is weighted so that this comprises 25% of total marks for the whole examination.

Writing: Questions 1–5 carry one mark each. Question 6 is marked out of five; and Question 7/8 is marked out of 20. This gives a total of 30 which is weighted so that it represents 25% of total marks for the whole examination.

Preparing for the Reading component

To prepare for the Reading component, you should read a variety of authentic texts, for example, newspapers and magazines, non-fiction books, and other sources of factual material, such as leaflets, brochures and websites. It is also a good idea to practise reading (and writing) short communicative messages, including notes, cards and emails. Remember, you won't always need to understand every word in order to be able to do a task in the exam.

Before the examination, think about the time you need to do each part. It is usually approximately 50 minutes on the Reading component and 40 minutes on the Writing component.

Reading			
Part	Task Type and Format	Task Focus	Number of Questions
1	Three-option multiple choice. Five short discrete texts: signs and messages, postcards, notes, emails, labels, etc., plus one example.	Reading real-world notices and other short texts for the main message.	5
2	Matching. Five items in the form of descriptions of people to match to eight short adapted-authentic texts.	Reading multiple texts for specific information and detailed comprehension.	5
3	True/False. Ten items with an adapted-authentic long text.	Processing a factual text. Scanning for specific information while disregarding redundant material.	10
4	Four-option multiple choice. Five items with an adapted-authentic long text.	Reading for detailed comprehension: understanding attitude, opinion and writer purpose. Reading for gist, inference and global meaning.	5
5	Four-option multiple-choice cloze. Ten items, plus an integrated example, with an adapted-authentic text drawn from a variety of sources. The text is of a factual or narrative nature.	Understanding of vocabulary and grammar in a short text, and understanding the lexico-structural patterns in the text.	10

A Guide to Cambridge English: Preliminary

Preparing for the Writing component

Part 1

You have to complete five sentences which will test your grammar. There is an example, showing exactly what the task involves. You should write between one and three words to fill this gap. The second sentence, when complete, must mean the same as the first sentence.

It is essential to spell correctly and no marks will be given if a word is misspelled. You will also lose the mark if you produce an answer of more than three words, even if your writing includes the correct answer.

Part 2

You have to produce a short communicative message of between 35 and 45 words in length. You are told who you are writing to and why, and you must include three content points. These are clearly laid out with bullet points in the question. To gain top marks, all three points must be in your answer, so it is important to read the question carefully and plan what you will include. Marks will not be deducted for minor errors.

Before the exam, you need to practise writing answers of the correct length. Answers that are too short or too long and likely to contain irrelevant information, will probably lose marks.

The General Mark Scheme below is used with a Task-specific Mark Scheme (see pages 106, 121, 136 and 151).

General Mark Scheme for Writing Part 2

Mark	Criteria	
5	All three parts of the message clearly communicated. Only minor spelling errors or occasional grammatical errors.	
4	All three parts of the message communicated. Some non-impeding errors in spelling or grammar, or some awkwardness of expression.	
3	All three parts of the message attempted. Expression requires interpretation by the reader and contains impeding errors in spelling and grammar.	Two parts of the message clearly communicated. Only minor spelling errors or occasional grammatical errors.
2	Only two parts of the message communicated. Some errors in spelling and grammar. The errors in expression may require patience and interpretation by the reader and impede communication.	
1	Only one part of the message communicated.	
0	Question unattempted, or totally incomprehensible response.	

Part 3

You have a choice of task: either a story or an informal letter. You need to write about 100 words.

Make sure you practise enough before the exam. Reading simplified readers in English will give you ideas for story writing. Also writing to a penfriend or e-pal will give you useful practice.

A Guide to Cambridge English: Preliminary

Mark Scheme for Writing Part 3

Examiners look at four aspects of your writing: Content, Communicative Achievement, Organisation, and Language.

Content focuses on how well you have fulfilled the task, in other words if you have done what you were asked to do.

Communicative Achievement focuses on how appropriate the writing is for the letter or story and whether you have used the appropriate register.

Organisation focuses on the way you put the piece of writing together, in other words if it is logical and ordered, and the punctuation is correct.

Language focuses on your vocabulary and grammar. This includes the range of language, as well as how accurate it is.

For each of the subscales, the examiner gives a maximum of five marks; this gives an overall maximum score of 20 for the Part 3 task.

Examiners use the following assessment scale:

B1	Content	Communicative Achievement	Organisation	Language
5	All content is relevant to the task. Target reader is fully informed.	Uses the conventions of the communicative task to hold the target reader's attention and communicate straightforward ideas.	Text is generally well organised and coherent, using a variety of linking words and cohesive devices.	Uses a range of everyday vocabulary appropriately, with occasional inappropriate use of less common lexis. Uses a range of simple and some complex grammatical forms with a good degree of control. Errors do not impede communication.
4	*Performance shares features of Bands 3 and 5.*			
3	Minor irrelevances and/or omissions may be present. Target reader is on the whole informed.	Uses the conventions of the communicative task in generally appropriate ways to communicate straightforward ideas.	Text is connected and coherent, using basic linking words and a limited number of cohesive devices.	Uses everyday vocabulary generally appropriately, while occasionally overusing certain lexis. Uses simple grammatical forms with a good degree of control. While errors are noticeable, meaning can still be determined.
2	*Performance shares features of Bands 1 and 3.*			
1	Irrelevances and misinterpretation of task may be present. Target reader is minimally informed.	Produces text that communicates simple ideas in simple ways.	Text is connected using basic, high-frequency linking words.	Uses basic vocabulary reasonably appropriately. Uses simple grammatical forms with some degree of control. Errors may impede meaning at times.

B1	Content	Communicative Achievement	Organisation	Language
0	Content is totally irrelevant. Target reader is not informed.	Performance below Band 1.		

Length of responses
Make sure you write the correct amount of words. Responses which are too short may not have an adequate range of language and may not provide all the information that is required. Responses which are too long may contain irrelevant content and have a negative effect on the reader.

Varieties of English
You are expected to use a particular variety of English with some degree of consistency in areas such as spelling, and not for example switch from using a British spelling of a word to an American spelling of the same word.

Writing			
Part	Task Type and Format	Task Focus	Number of Questions
1	Sentence transformations. Five items, plus an integrated example, that are theme-related. Candidates are given sentences and then asked to complete similar sentences using a different structural pattern so that the sentence still has the same meaning.	Control and understanding of *Threshold/Cambridge English: Preliminary* grammatical structures. Rephrasing and reformulating information.	5
2	Short communicative message. Candidates are prompted to write a short message in the form of a postcard, note, email, etc. The prompt takes the form of a rubric to respond to.	A short piece of writing of 35–45 words focusing on communication of specific messages.	1
3	A longer piece of continuous writing. There is a choice of two questions, an informal letter or a story. Candidates are assessed on four aspects of their writing: Content, Communication Achievement, Organisation, and Language.	Writing about 100 words focusing on control and range of language.	1

Paper 2: Listening

Paper format
This paper contains four parts.

Number of questions
25

Text types
All texts are based on authentic situations.

Answering

Candidates indicate answers either by shading lozenges (Parts 1, 2 and 4) or writing answers (Part 3) on an answer sheet. Candidates record their answers on the question paper as they listen. They are then given six minutes at the end of the test to copy these on to the answer sheet.

Recording information

Each text is heard twice. Recordings will contain a variety of accents corresponding to standard variants of native speaker accents.

Timing

About 35 minutes, including six minutes to transfer answers.

Marks

Each question carries one mark. This gives a total of 25 marks, which represents 25% of total marks for the whole examination.

Part	Task Type and Format	Task Focus	Number of questions
1	Multiple choice (discrete). Short neutral or informal monologues or dialogues. Seven discrete three-option multiple-choice items with visuals, plus one example.	Listening to identify key information from short exchanges.	7
2	Multiple choice. Longer monologue or interview (with one main speaker). Six three-option multiple-choice items.	Listening to identify specific information and detailed meaning.	6
3	Gap-fill. Longer monologue. Six gaps to fill in. Candidates need to write one or more words in each space.	Listening to identify, understand and interpret information.	6
4	True/False. Longer informal dialogue. Candidates need to decide whether six statements are correct or incorrect.	Listening for detailed meaning, and to identify the attitudes and opinions of the speakers.	6

Preparing for the Listening paper

You will hear the instructions for each task on the recording, and see them on the exam paper. In Part 1, there is also an example text and task to show you how to record your answers.
In Parts 2, 3 and 4, the instructions are followed by a pause; you should read the questions in that part then. This will help you prepare for the listening.

The best preparation for the Listening paper is to listen to authentic spoken English at this level. Having discussions provides a good authentic source of listening practice, as does listening to the teacher. You can also listen to texts to give you practice in understanding different voices and styles of delivery.

A Guide to Cambridge English: Preliminary

Paper 3: Speaking

Paper format
The standard format is two candidates and two examiners. One of the examiners acts as an interlocutor and the other as an assessor. The interlocutor directs the test, while the assessor takes no part in the interaction.

Timing
10–12 minutes per pair of candidates.

Marks
Candidates are assessed on their performance throughout the test. There are a total of 25 marks in Paper 3, making 25% of the total score for the whole examination.

Part	Task Type and Format	Task Focus	Timing
1	Each candidate interacts with the interlocutor. The interlocutor asks the candidates questions in turn, using standardised questions.	Giving information of a factual, personal kind. The candidates respond to questions about present circumstances, past experiences and future plans.	2–3 minutes
2	Simulated situation. Candidates interact with each other. Visual stimulus is given to the candidates to aid the discussion task. The interlocutor sets up the activity using a standardised rubric.	Using functional language to make and respond to suggestions, discuss alternatives, make recommendations and negotiate agreement.	2–3 minutes
3	Extended turn. A colour photograph is given to each candidate in turn and they are asked to talk about it for up to a minute. Both photographs relate to the same topic.	Describing photographs and managing discourse, using appropriate vocabulary, in a longer turn.	3 minutes
4	General conversation. Candidates interact with each other. The topic of the conversation develops the theme established in Part 3. The interlocutor sets up the activity using a standardised rubric.	The candidates talk together about their opinions, likes/dislikes, preferences, experiences, habits, etc.	3 minutes

Assessment
Throughout the Speaking test, examiners listen to what you say and give you marks for how well you speak English, so you must try to speak about the tasks and answer the examiner and your partner's questions.

You are awarded marks by two examiners; the assessor and the interlocutor. The assessor awards marks from the Analytical Assessment scales for the following criteria:

Grammar and Vocabulary
This refers to how accurately you use grammar and also to the correct use of vocabulary. It also includes how wide a range of grammar and vocabulary you use.

Discourse Management

This refers to the length, relevance and coherence of your answers. You should be able to produce sentences which are clear and easy to follow. What you say should be related to the topic and the conversation in general.

Pronunciation

This refers to the how easy it is to understand what you say. You should be able to say words and sentences that are easy to understand.

Interactive Communication

This refers to how well you can talk about the task and to your partner and the examiner. You should be able to start the conversation and keep it going, and ask for repetition or clarification if needed.

B1	Grammar and Vocabulary	Discourse Management	Pronunciation	Interactive Communication
5	Shows a good degree of control of simple grammatical forms, and attempts some complex grammatical forms. Uses a range of appropriate vocabulary to give and exchange views on familiar topics.	Produces extended stretches of language despite some hesitation. Contributions are relevant despite some repetition. Uses a range of cohesive devices.	Is intelligible. Intonation is generally appropriate. Sentence and word stress is generally accurately placed. Individual sounds are generally articulated clearly.	Initiates and responds appropriately. Maintains and develops the interaction and negotiates towards an outcome with very little support.
4	*Performance shares features of Bands 3 and 5.*			
3	Shows a good degree of control of simple grammatical forms. Uses a range of appropriate vocabulary when talking about familiar topics.	Produces responses which are extended beyond short phrases, despite hesitation. Contributions are mostly relevant, but there may be some repetition. Uses basic cohesive devices.	Is mostly intelligible, and has some control of phonological features at both utterance and word levels.	Initiates and responds appropriately. Keeps the interaction going with very little prompting and support.
2	*Performance shares features of Bands 1 and 3.*			
1	Shows sufficient control of simple grammatical forms. Uses a limited range of appropriate vocabulary to talk about familiar topics.	Produces responses which are characterised by short phrases and frequent hesitation. Repeats information or digresses from the topic.	Is mostly intelligible, despite limited control of phonological features.	Maintains simple exchanges, despite some difficulty. Requires prompting and support.
0	*Performance below Band 1.*			

The examiner asking the questions (the interlocutor) gives marks for how well you do overall using a Global Achievement scale.

B1	Global Achievement
5	Handles communication on familiar topics, despite some hesitation. Organises extended discourse but occasionally produces utterances that lack coherence, and some inaccuracies and inappropriate usage occur.
4	*Performance shares features of Bands 3 and 5.*
3	Handles communication in everyday situations, despite hesitation. Constructs longer utterances but is not able to use complex language except in well-rehearsed utterances.
2	*Performance shares features of Bands 1 and 3.*
1	Conveys basic meaning in very familiar everyday situations. Produces utterances which tend to be very short – words or phrases – with frequent hesitation and pauses.
0	*Performance below Band 1.*

Further information

More information about *Cambridge English: Preliminary* or any other Cambridge ESOL examination can be obtained from Cambridge ESOL at the address below or from the website at www.CambridgeESOL.org

University of Cambridge ESOL Examinations
1 Hills Road
Cambridge CB1 2EU
United Kingdom

Telephone +44 1223 553997
Fax: +44 1223 553621
email: ESOLHelpdesk@CambridgeESOL.org

Test 1

PAPER 1 READING AND WRITING TEST (1 hour 30 minutes)

READING

Part 1

Questions 1–5

Look at the text in each question.
What does it say?
Mark the correct letter **A**, **B** or **C** on your answer sheet.

Example:

0

Nothing of value is left in this van at night

A Valuable objects are removed at night.

B Valuables should not be left in the van.

C This van is locked at night.

Answer: | 0 | A B C |

1

Road repairs starting here on 1st September for four weeks — expect delays

A This part of the road will open again on 1st September.

B Your journey may take longer on this road in September.

C We are expecting more traffic on this road in September.

2

Welcome to Hotel Maroc

Dear Guest

Our holiday advisor is available in the lounge every day 8–10 am for booking guided tours, museum/garden tickets, camel rides.

Enjoy your stay!

A People staying at Hotel Maroc can arrange activities through the hotel.

B Hotel Maroc's holiday advisor accompanies guests on tours.

C Daily sightseeing trips start from the Hotel Maroc.

3

Online Booking Form

Name ....
Address ....
No. of tickets ....

Tickets booked within seven days of a performance are kept for collection.

A Tickets will be sent to you within seven days of booking.

B When booking, advise staff if your tickets are to be kept for collection.

C We don't post tickets booked one week or less before the performance.

4

New Message

To: All players
From: Paul

The team is the same as last week – I've already checked everyone can play. Anyone needing a lift to Fyfield can phone me.

A Players who have a problem getting to the Fyfield match should contact Paul.

B Anyone who wants to play in the Fyfield game needs to speak to Paul.

C Team members who are not available for the Fyfield match must phone Paul.

5

IMPROVED SERVICE:

From next month this bank will remain open until 2 pm on Saturdays

A After next month the bank will be open all weekend.

B The bank closes at 2 pm on weekdays.

C The bank will have longer opening hours in future.

Test 1

Part 2

Questions 6–10

The people below all want to watch a television programme.
On the opposite page there are descriptions of eight television programmes.
Decide which programme would be the most suitable for the following people.
For questions **6–10**, mark the correct letter (**A–H**) on your answer sheet.

---

6 Sandrine and her ten-year-old daughter, Daisy, love watching all kinds of dancing, especially if the dancers are famous entertainers. Daisy particularly likes the beautiful dresses the women wear.

7 Tim has an amazing memory for facts on a range of topics. He enjoys testing himself against people taking part in quizzes on TV and wants to find out how to be on one himself.

8 Simon enjoys murder mysteries, and likes the challenge of working out who did the crime before the identity of the murderer is uncovered in the final scene.

9 Mariella loves skiing and enjoys watching winter sports on television. She tries to improve her techniques by copying the professionals who take part in them.

10 Ned and Jake are computer programmers. They enjoy TV programmes that are funny and give them a complete break from their work, especially if they are connected with football.

ON TV TONIGHT

A Below stairs
New comedy series about Ray and Jen, who work in the IT section of a big company. Their office is in the basement while their bosses work in luxury upstairs. Reviews so far have been mixed. There are plenty of laughs, though some people may find the situations rather silly.

B Whiteout
All the latest action from the slopes, including men's and women's downhill racing, jumping, ice dance and ice hockey. Presented from the mountains by former footballer Neville Gray, with expert reports on speeds and distances. Figure skater Jayne Wilton comments on the dance performances.

C Top Team
A return of the jokey quiz show, in which teams of famous sports personalities and comedians have to give amusing answers to questions on a range of popular sports, not just football and tennis but winter sports too. Light-hearted entertainment for everyone!

D Quicksteps
Each week, well-known faces from the world of television team up with a professional partner to perform a range of classical and modern dances. You, the viewer, can vote for the best performance and the best costume, and each week's winners will take part in the grand final later in the year.

E Taskmaster
Can you beat the four members of the public who answer general knowledge and specialist questions in the final of this year's competition? Tonight's specialist subjects include the history of winter sports, Latin American dances, detective novels and French history. There will be information about how to enter next year's competition.

F The Two Dancers
Set in late 18th-century France, this drama tells of the relationship between two beautiful dancers who both love the same man. Although the ending is not unexpected, this drama is thoroughly entertaining all the way through. Worth watching just for the beautiful costumes and scenery.

G Inspector Blake
A first-division football player has a beautiful wife, a big house and a bright future. When he's found dead in his car near a local park, Blake discovers that he was less popular than it seemed. Set in the 1970s, this nail-biting drama will keep you guessing right until the end.

H Madison
This little-known musical is based on the true story of an American ice hockey team in the 1930s. The facts are historically accurate, even though the show is advertised as a musical comedy-thriller. Really only of interest to experts in the history of musicals or ice hockey fans.

Test 1

Part 3

Questions 11–20

Look at the sentences below about a man who got lost in the Rocky Mountains.
Read the text on the opposite page to decide if each sentence is correct or incorrect.
If it is correct, mark **A** on your answer sheet.
If it is not correct, mark **B** on your answer sheet.

11   Bob Rigsby was in Canada in order to study its wildlife.

12   On the first day of getting lost, Bob realised how serious his situation was.

13   Bob had few problems finding something safe to eat in the mountains.

14   On the fourth day, Bob recognised the place that he was in.

15   Shirley thought that Bob sounded upset on the phone.

16   It was the first time Bob had been missing for such a length of time.

17   The first phone call that Shirley made was to the Canadian embassy.

18   The hotel owner was worried while Bob was absent from the hotel.

19   Employees from the hotel went to look for Bob.

20   Bob says he regrets going into the mountains on his own.

Lost in the Rocky Mountains

Fifty-four-year-old scientist Bob Rigsby was lost for five days in Canada's Rocky Mountains, and was only rescued after a mobile phone call to his wife, Shirley, over 8,000 km away in England.

Bob, a British wildlife expert, had been in Vancouver, Canada, giving a talk at a conference on the environment. When it was over, he travelled to the Rocky Mountains and checked into The Maple Leaf hotel. He then set off on a short walk to look at the local plant and animal life. After a couple of hours, he realised he had taken a wrong turning on the mountain path, but was sure he could easily get back to the hotel. Even when night fell, he remained confident.

But, after walking for several hours the next day, it became clear to Bob that he was in trouble. 'I had my mobile phone with me, but the battery was almost dead. I thought I could probably make just one call but I didn't know the number of my hotel and I didn't want to worry my family unless I really had to.' Bob carried on walking for three more days. He knew which wild plants he could safely eat and he had little trouble finding them. When he was thirsty he drank from streams.

On the fourth day, he reached a forest that he knew he had walked through the previous day. His heart sank. He realised it was hopeless and decided to call his family in England. 'He was quite calm when he spoke to me on the phone,' says Shirley. 'He appeared to be in control of the situation, in spite of everything. He'd been lost a few times before, but never for so many days – that's why this time was different.' She immediately contacted The Maple Leaf hotel, after a quick call to the Canadian embassy in London to get its phone number. 'We're always anxious if our guests are away for a long time,' says Greg McCaffrey, the hotel's owner. 'But that week several of our English visitors had gone to the city for a few days to watch the hockey games, and we thought Mr Rigsby had gone too.' As soon as Shirley phoned, hotel staff called the rescue service, who sent out a search party for the scientist. They found him in a cave some hours later, very tired, but, apart from some cuts and scratches, quite unhurt.

'I've learnt my lesson,' says Bob. 'I admit I was stupid to set off like that without a guide. I never want an experience like that again!'

Test 1

Part 4

Questions 21–25

Read the text and questions below.
For each question, mark the correct letter **A**, **B**, **C** or **D** on your answer sheet.

Open-air Theatre

In Britain, the ancient tradition of open-air performances is still alive and well. Cornwall has some of Britain's oldest working theatres, with one open-air theatre actually built into a cliff, a project only recently completed.

Two actors, Dave James and Muriel Thomas, came from London theatres to join a theatre company called Coastline. They now regularly perform in just such a theatre, by the sea. 'One thing about performing outside is we never know what'll happen. For example, if a bird lands on stage, we can't act as if it's not there – the audience are all watching it. So we just bring the bird into the play, too. Once, about 30 dolphins came past, jumping out of the water and showing off. The audience were all chatting about them instead of watching the play, so the actors just gave up for a while and watched the dolphins, too.'

The weather can also be difficult. 'Sometimes it's been so bad,' says Muriel, 'that we've asked the audience if they really want to stay. But usually they sit with their coats and umbrellas and say, "Yes, please carry on!" They must feel it isn't much fun, but no one's returned their ticket so far!'

Coastline's director, John Barnack, works hard to introduce people to theatre. 'Many people think of theatres as clubs where they don't belong and are not welcome,' he explains. 'Sitting in the open air changes that feeling. The audience are far more involved – they aren't sitting in the dark, at a distance like in normal theatres, and that improves the actors' performances, too. I'm very proud of the work they've done so far.'

21 What is the writer trying to do in the text?

- **A** follow the development of open-air theatre in Britain
- **B** describe how one open-air theatre was built
- **C** explain what it's like to work in an open-air theatre
- **D** warn readers about the disadvantages of attending open-air performances

Reading

22 When plays are disturbed by local wildlife, the actors

- **A** change their performance to include it.
- **B** carry on as though nothing had happened.
- **C** stop and have a chat with the audience.
- **D** cancel the rest of the performance.

23 What is the audience's attitude to bad weather during performances?

- **A** They worry about the actors getting wet.
- **B** They say that it stops them enjoying the play.
- **C** They accept it as they have come well-prepared.
- **D** They feel they should have their money back.

24 What does John Barnack say about outdoor theatre?

- **A** He's afraid the atmosphere is more stressful for actors.
- **B** He's happy that the audience feel comfortable being there.
- **C** He's worried that it creates an atmosphere similar to a club.
- **D** He welcomes the distance it creates between actors and audience.

25 What would an actor from the Coastline company write in his or her diary?

A A difficult performance today – it was pouring with rain. Luckily the audience couldn't see my face in the dark. . .

B The theatre looks so old it's hard to imagine they've just finished it. I'd prefer to be by the sea while I'm performing, though. . .

C I'm glad I moved from the London theatre scene. But I don't think our director is satisfied with what we've done so far. . .

D I'm keeping a tradition going, and it tests my acting skills, as I never know what unexpected things I'll have to deal with. . .

21

Test 1

Part 5

Questions 26–35

Read the text below and choose the correct word for each space.
For each question, mark the correct letter **A**, **B**, **C** or **D** on your answer sheet.

Example:

0   **A** was   **B** is   **C** has   **D** had

Answer: 0 [A■ B☐ C☐ D☐]

Alexander Graham Bell

Alexander Graham Bell **(0)** .... born in Scotland in 1847. His father, an expert on speech, **(26)** .... a way of teaching how words **(27)** .... be pronounced. He translated the **(28)** .... of words into straight or curvy lines.

Alexander **(29)** .... to be a teacher and, when his mother went deaf, he started to be **(30)** .... in how deaf people communicate. In 1870, because his children were in poor health, Alexander and his family moved to the United States. He hoped that a warmer **(31)** .... would be better for the whole family. It was while he was teaching deaf children there **(32)** .... he invented a new machine. It was very **(33)** .... to the human ear itself, and Bell discovered it could carry human speech **(34)** .... a wire from one place to another. It was not long before the telephone was a part of **(35)** .... our lives!

26	**A** grew	**B** built	**C** developed	**D** worked
27	**A** ought	**B** should	**C** might	**D** would
28	**A** calls	**B** voices	**C** noises	**D** sounds
29	**A** trained	**B** became	**C** educated	**D** taught
30	**A** amazed	**B** interested	**C** surprised	**D** excited
31	**A** geography	**B** season	**C** climate	**D** weather
32	**A** so	**B** because	**C** since	**D** that
33	**A** likely	**B** similar	**C** same	**D** accurate
34	**A** above	**B** about	**C** along	**D** around
35	**A** any	**B** each	**C** all	**D** every

WRITING

Part 1

Questions 1–5

Here are some sentences about the Santiago Bernabéu football stadium in Spain.
For each question, complete the second sentence so that it means the same as the first.
Use no more than three words.
Write only the missing words on your answer sheet.
You may use this page for any rough work.

Example:

0   The Santiago Bernabéu stadium is close to the centre of Madrid.

   The Santiago Bernabéu stadium is not .... the centre of Madrid.

Answer: | 0 | far from |

---

1   Last week, one of my friends visited the Santiago Bernabéu football stadium.

   Last week, a friend of .... visited the Santiago Bernabéu football stadium.

2   He had not been to this stadium before.

   It .... the first time he had been to this stadium.

3   It costs €9 to go on a tour of the stadium.

   You have to .... €9 to go on a tour of the stadium.

4   A visit to the dressing room is included in the tour.

   The tour .... a visit to the dressing room.

5   No other football stadium in Madrid is as big as Santiago Bernabéu.

   Santiago Bernabéu is .... any other football stadium in Madrid.

23

Test 1

Part 2

Question 6

You've just bought something new for your bedroom.

Write an email to your friend Teresa. In your email, you should

- describe what you have bought
- explain why you needed it
- say where you're going to put it.

Write **35–45 words** on your answer sheet.

Writing

Part 3

Write an answer to **one** of the questions (**7** or **8**) in this part.
Write your answer in about **100 words** on your answer sheet.
Tick the box (Question 7 or Question 8) on your answer sheet to show which question you have answered.

Question 7

- This is part of a letter you receive from an English friend.

> I enjoy my new job but I sit at a computer all day now. I don't get much exercise. What do you think I should do to keep fit?

- Now write a letter, giving your friend some advice about keeping fit.
- Write your **letter** in about 100 words on your answer sheet.

Question 8

- Your English teacher has asked you to write a story.
- Your story must begin with this sentence:

When I sat down, I discovered I was next to someone very famous.

- Write your **story** in about 100 words on your answer sheet.

25

Test 1

PAPER 2 LISTENING TEST approx 35 minutes
(including 6 minutes transfer time)

Part 1

Questions 1–7

There are seven questions in this part.
For each question there are three pictures and a short recording.
Choose the correct picture and put a tick (✓) in the box below it.

Example: Where is the girl's hat?

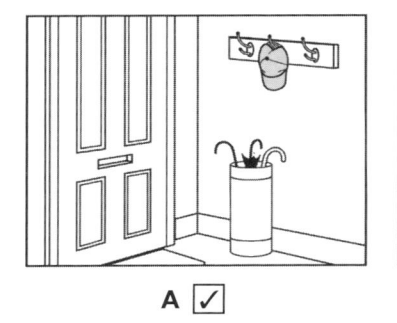

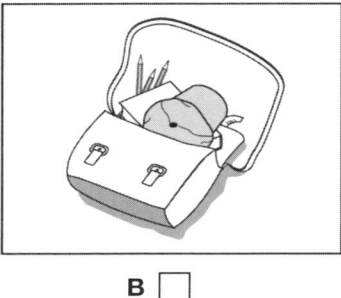

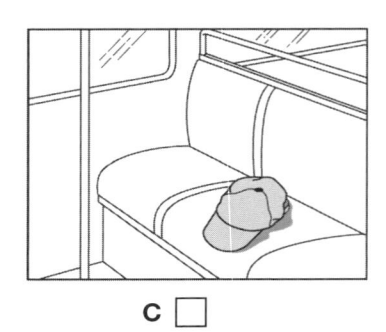

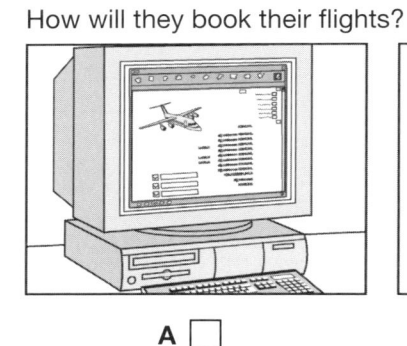

A ✓   B ☐   C ☐

1 How will they book their flights?

A ☐   B ☐   C ☐

2 What has the daughter forgotten to bring on holiday?

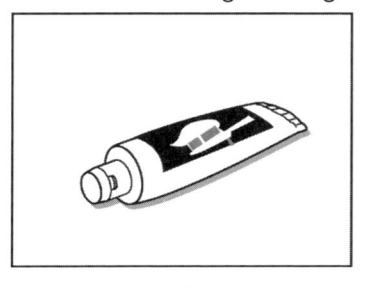

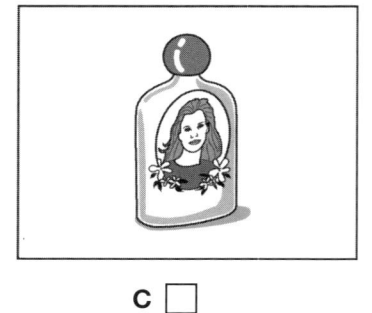

A ☐   B ☐   C ☐

26

Listening

3 What will the man and woman do on Sunday?

A ☐   B ☐   C ☐

4 Which blouse does the girl decide to buy?

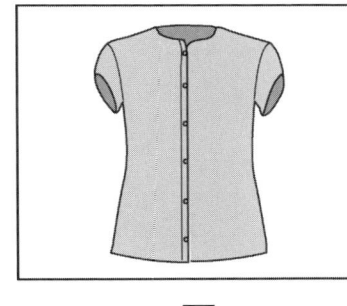

A ☐   B ☐   C ☐

5 When is the girl having a party?

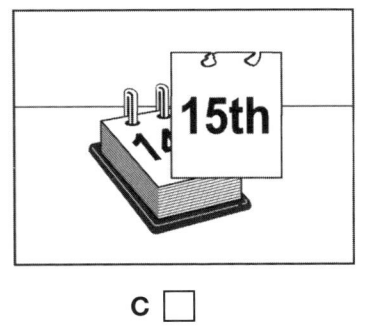

A ☐   B ☐   C ☐

27

Test 1

6 Where is the motorcycle race going to finish?

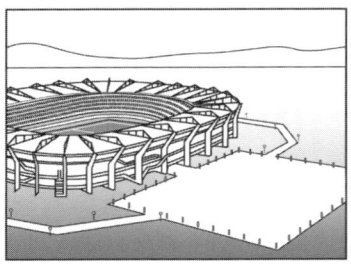

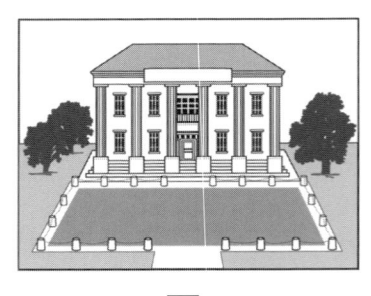

A ☐ B ☐ C ☐

7 What will the woman repair next?

A ☐ B ☐ C ☐

Listening

Part 2

Questions 8–13

You will hear a radio interview with a man called Robin Marshall, who has written a book about Argentina.
For each question, put a tick (✓) in the correct box.

---

8 What was Robin's job in Argentina?

A ☐ translator
B ☐ tour guide
C ☐ travelling salesman

9 On Robin's last trip to Argentina, the weather was

A ☐ colder than he expected.
B ☐ suitable for what he planned.
C ☐ different from the forecasts he heard.

10 What did Robin buy from the market he visited?

A ☐ a picture
B ☐ a chair
C ☐ a record

11 How did Robin feel during the dance performance he saw?

A ☐ He wanted to get up and dance.
B ☐ He wished he had continued his dance classes.
C ☐ He was sad he didn't dance well.

Test 1

12 What did Robin do while he stayed in the village?
   A ☐ He went on a bus tour.
   B ☐ He went into the forest.
   C ☐ He went on a river trip.

13 What did Robin like about his favourite place?
   A ☐ the wildlife
   B ☐ the views
   C ☐ the peace

Part 3

Questions 14–19

You will hear a radio presenter talking about a museum where you can see a new film. For each question, fill in the missing information in the numbered space.

FILM AT THE SCIENCE MUSEUM

The Film

Country it is about: **(14)** ....

Day it is on: Sunday

Time last performance starts: **(15)** ....

Other things to do at the museum

— use the **(16)** .... in the basement

— see a model **(17)** .... on the first floor

— try the café on the **(18)** .... floor

How to get free tickets for the film

— send an email before 12 o'clock on **(19)** ....

Test 1

Part 4

Questions 20–25

Look at the six sentences for this part.
You will hear two neighbours, a woman, Natasha, and a man, Colin, talking about running.
Decide if each sentence is correct or incorrect.
If it is correct, put a tick (✓) in the box under **A** for **YES**. If it is not correct, put a tick (✓) in the box under **B** for **NO**.

		A YES	B NO
20	Natasha has decided to take the day off work to go running.	☐	☐
21	Colin found running to work was bad for his health.	☐	☐
22	Natasha would prefer to go running outside the city.	☐	☐
23	Natasha would like to wear her sports clothes at work.	☐	☐
24	Natasha will run in the big race because she hopes to win it.	☐	☐
25	Colin and Natasha will prepare for the big race together.	☐	☐

About the Speaking test

The Speaking test lasts about 10 to 12 minutes. You take the test with another candidate. There are two examiners in the room. One examiner talks to you and the other examiner listens to you. Both the examiners give you marks.

Part 1

The examiners introduce themselves and then one examiner asks you and your partner to say your names and spell them. This examiner then asks you questions about yourself, your daily life, interests, etc.

Part 2

The examiner asks you to talk about something together and gives you a drawing to help you.

Part 3

You each have a chance to talk by yourselves. The examiner gives you a colour photograph to look at and asks you to talk about it. When you have finished talking, the examiner gives your partner a different photograph to look at and to talk about.

Part 4

The examiner asks you and your partner to say more about the subject of the photographs in Part 3. You may be asked to give your opinion or to talk about something that has happened to you.

Test 2

PAPER 1   READING AND WRITING TEST   (1 hour 30 minutes)

READING

Part 1

Questions 1–5

Look at the text in each question.
What does it say?
Mark the correct letter **A**, **B** or **C** on your answer sheet.

Example:

0   **REGENCY CAMERAS**
    Buy two films and get one FREE

A   Buy three films for the price of two.

B   Get a free film with every one you buy.

C   Films bought here are printed free.

Answer: 0 A B C

---

1   Mum,
    The tennis team's meeting tonight, so I'm taking my tennis clothes for the photo – can't wait to see myself in it.
    Daniel

A   Daniel is having his photo taken with the tennis team tonight.

B   Daniel needs his tennis clothes to play in a match tonight.

C   Daniel is taking a photo of the rest of the tennis team tonight.

34

2

Casali Restaurant

We are open downstairs while improvements are made to this area.

A Please come downstairs and try our recently improved restaurant.

B The restaurant will reopen when the improvements are finished.

C You can only eat in one part of the restaurant at the moment.

3

Ann-Marie,
Emma called. She's got a free ticket for this evening's concert as her boyfriend's busy. I've already got one, but if you want to go, call her before 7 pm.
Joe

A Joe and Emma should decide whether they want the spare ticket.

B If Ann-Marie is free, she could go to the same concert as Joe tonight.

C Ann-Marie phoned to offer Emma her ticket to a concert.

4

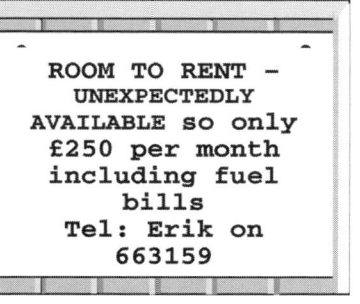

ROOM TO RENT –
UNEXPECTEDLY
AVAILABLE so only
£250 per month
including fuel
bills
Tel: Erik on
663159

A People renting this room should expect to pay extra for gas and electricity.

B The rent for this room is reduced to £250 plus bills.

C This room is cheap to rent as it was not expected to be empty.

5

New Message
From: Maria Gomez
To: Sarah Smith

Please forgive the delay in writing – I've been so busy!

I miss your English classes now I'm back in Spain, but at least I can understand everything here!

In this email, Maria wants to

A explain why she hasn't contacted Sarah Smith before.

B tell Sarah Smith how much her English has improved.

C thank Sarah Smith for her English classes in Spain.

Test 2

Part 2

Questions 6–10

The people below all want to go to a skiing holiday centre.
On the opposite page there are descriptions of eight skiing holiday centres.
Decide which skiing holiday centre would be the most suitable for the following people.
For questions **6–10**, mark the correct letter (**A–H**) on your answer sheet.

6   Tomoko hasn't skied before and wants inexpensive lessons from a teacher who speaks Japanese or English. She'd like to stay somewhere where she doesn't have to cook for herself.

7   Alex and Helen are going skiing for the second time and would like a centre with easy skiing and interesting places to visit. They want to fly there and rent skis cheaply on arrival.

8   Matt and Martin are looking for some exciting skiing. They don't want to be with beginners or worry that there might not be enough snow. They like eating out in the evenings.

9   Isabel and her 14-year-old son, Juan, are expert skiers but her husband is a beginner. Juan would like to try other winter sports, like snowboarding. They'll travel to the holiday centre by train.

10   Chris and his wife Jo are not keen skiers. They want to be able to relax in the sun and admire the beautiful scenery while their sons of 10 and 12 have skiing lessons.

36

SKIING HOLIDAY CENTRES

A Windy Pine
The ski and snowboard runs here are high in the mountains so you can be sure of lots of good snow, but they are extremely challenging and only for the expert. Skiers can relax after dark in a number of small bars and restaurants. The airport is a two-hour bus ride away.

B Mount Brock
This centre is family-friendly with lots of sporting activities for children, but there isn't much to interest advanced skiers. Although there's seldom a lack of snow on Mount Brock, it can be cloudy so that the scenery is hidden. Access is by road.

C Ice Mountain
Come to this beautiful spot if you're new to the sport. Try out easy ski runs under the instruction of qualified teachers – their services are reasonably priced and many speak several languages including English. Classes are for adults only. Guesthouses provide accommodation with breakfast and evening meals. The centre is reached by train.

D Eagle's Nest
There's skiing in this area for skiers of all abilities, with special classes for children, but snowboarders aren't welcome. Accommodation is in comfortable holiday apartments with balconies, where non-skiers can enjoy the fine weather surrounded by wonderful mountain views. There's a good bus service from the centre to the nearest train station.

E Bear Point
This centre is a favourite with skilful young skiers who have limited money. Accommodation is reasonably priced and there's a variety of evening entertainment. However, it's hard to find a good instructor and you can't be certain of the snowfall. Cheap flights go to the local airport.

F Rose Valley
This area has much to offer, both to skiers with little or no experience and to those wanting challenging and exciting skiing. Ski instructors speak French and German. Some slopes are reserved for snowboarders. There's lively nightlife but the weather can be unreliable. Access to the area is by rail.

G Mount David
There's good open skiing here, without too many twists and turns, making it suitable for intermediate skiers. Equipment hire is expensive. Accommodation is of a high standard and there are excellent restaurants, but prices are high. The airport isn't far away.

H Fairview
This historic mountain town has much for visitors to see. The slopes don't attract expert skiers, but are suitable for those wishing to improve their basic skills. English-speaking instructors charge a lot, but hiring equipment is very reasonable. This centre isn't recommended for children. The airport is nearby.

Test 2

Part 3

Questions 11–20

Look at the sentences below about a music day for young people.
Read the text on the opposite page to decide if each sentence is correct or incorrect.
If it is correct, mark **A** on your answer sheet.
If it is not correct, mark **B** on your answer sheet.

---

11 The aim of the music day is for young professional musicians to meet each other.

12 Students will learn some music to play to an audience in the evening.

13 At the concert, the professional musicians will perform individually.

14 Transport home by coach from the concert hall will be provided.

15 Classes will begin straight after the students have registered.

16 Each student attending may be lucky enough to be taught individually.

17 Students wanting any of the goods on sale can collect their chosen items after the concert.

18 Students staying to wait for the evening concert are advised to take their own entertainment.

19 Some students will need to bring their evening clothes with them in the morning.

20 For safety reasons, the organisers want to know how many students will be at the concert.

Young People's Music Day

Dear Young Musicians,

Thank you for agreeing to take part in our Music Day. Here are some notes for your information.

The day
The whole idea of the day is for music students from secondary schools around the area to meet other players and receive expert teaching from our guests, six professional players. In the evening, you will perform the pieces you have worked on during the day at a concert which your friends and family can attend. The concert will include a range of music from you, followed by one piece from each of our guests.

Getting there
A map is included for the concert hall. Your school coaches will drop you at the main building. Please note that there is no return coach journey.

The programme
After you have registered at the reception, go to the main hall. First there will be a short performance by our professional musicians who are joining us for the day. After this you will go into your classes to practise on your own instruments for the evening concert. There will also be a chance to experiment with a different instrument from the one you normally play, and see if you enjoy playing something more unusual – we have several instruments to choose from!

What to bring
Bring a piece of music that you can play well. Part of the day will include a 'masterclass' in which you might have the opportunity, if there is enough time, to play a piece of your choosing and be given a short lesson by one of the professional players.

What to buy
There will be opportunities to buy sheet music or books during the day, so you may want to have money for these. If you wish to buy something, you could reserve it and then arrange to pick it up and pay when your parents arrive to watch the concert. This service will be available until 7 pm.

Going home
The first part of the day will finish at 5 pm, when parents can collect students. For those remaining in the hall until the evening concert at 7 pm, there will be DVDs for you to watch, although you should also bring something to do while you are waiting. A change of clothes is required for the evening – black trousers or skirt and white top – so unless you are going home at 5 pm, you will need to have this with you at the start of the day.

Evening concert
If for whatever reason you cannot attend the evening concert, you must inform us as soon as possible, as we need to know numbers in order to prepare the stage.

We look forward to seeing you at the Young People's Music Day.

Test 2

Part 4

Questions 21–25

Read the text and questions below.
For each question, mark the correct letter **A**, **B**, **C** or **D** on your answer sheet.

Rik Mayall talks about his experiences as an actor

I've enjoyed all the parts I've played, especially people who aren't very nice, such as Alan, the politician I played in the TV comedy series *The New Statesman*. Some people loved him, but there were others who were against the programme because they thought it was wrong to make jokes about politics on television. I haven't seen that series for years. I don't think they could repeat it because many of the jokes were from that time. Comedy does date sometimes, though the basic idea behind the series – a self-important person – can be true of any time.

I do a lot of film work and still enjoy playing funny characters on TV, but I prefer theatre. I need a live audience to keep me going. If I chose a favourite part, it would be Henri in *A Family Affair*, a play we performed up and down the country several years ago. It's a comedy, directed by Andy de la Tour, a good friend of mine. It's about a family who meet to celebrate a birthday, and all kinds of things happen – things that could happen to anyone, anywhere. That's why it's so funny.

I really liked playing the part of Henri because in some ways his character is similar to mine. Henri's a bit of a loner and behaves very badly at times. I was delighted when the authors of the play saw it and congratulated me, saying I was exactly as they'd imagined Henri. Although the play is a comedy, it contains serious messages, such as how thoughtless people can be. It's very true to life and that's why I like it.

---

21 What is Rik Mayall's main purpose in writing the text?

  A to suggest reasons for the success of his career
  B to explain how he became a comedy actor
  C to talk about his favourite acting roles
  D to describe his future work on television

22 What does Rik Mayall say about *The New Statesman*?

    A It won't be repeated because some people were upset.
    B Not everyone approved of it.
    C It was based on an unpleasant person he met.
    D He enjoys watching it again from time to time.

23 What kind of work does Rik Mayall prefer?

    A performing in front of an audience
    B acting with his close friends
    C doing comedy series for television
    D making films about real people

24 Why was Rik Mayall pleased about acting in *A Family Affair*?

    A He could insist on which character to play.
    B The writers of the play admired his performance.
    C It allowed him to do some serious acting.
    D He played a character who was very different to himself.

25 Which of the following is the best description of Rik Mayall?

    A He is a comedy actor who dislikes playing roles that are based on real life.

    B He is a well-known actor who has given up playing funny characters on TV in order to concentrate on serious theatre.

    C He is a famous actor who played in *A Family Affair* because he said it reminded him of his own family situation.

    D He is a successful actor who says that he enjoys playing characters who are unpleasant.

Test 2

Part 5

Questions 26–35

Read the text below and choose the correct word for each space.
For each question, mark the correct letter **A**, **B**, **C** or **D** on your answer sheet.

Example:

| 0 | **A** very | **B** so | **C** too | **D** such |

Answer: 0 **A** ■ B ☐ C ☐ D ☐

THE ART OF DRAWING

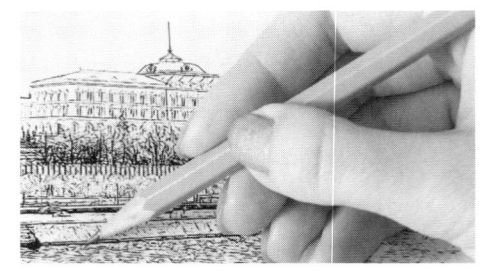

Drawing has always been a (0) .... popular hobby. Young children draw with a pencil as (26) .... as they can hold one. Drawing is often seen as a special skill, and it is (27) .... that some people seem to draw perfect pictures without any effort. Yet drawing, like writing, can be (28) .... ; you can draw accurately if you work really hard at it.

Drawing is first (29) .... all about looking carefully. It sounds easy to say that all you (30) .... to do is look at things, but it really is that simple. The best way to draw a familiar (31) .... is to imagine that you are looking at it for the first (32) ....

Nowadays there are (33) .... courses and materials available than ever before, (34) .... means that you can experiment to improve your skills. The only (35) .... is your imagination.

26	**A** fast	**B** immediately	**C** soon	**D** shortly
27	**A** true	**B** actual	**C** exact	**D** real
28	**A** discovered	**B** made	**C** learnt	**D** reached
29	**A** of	**B** in	**C** from	**D** for
30	**A** should	**B** need	**C** must	**D** could
31	**A** topic	**B** subject	**C** area	**D** person
32	**A** period	**B** term	**C** moment	**D** time
33	**A** more	**B** many	**C** plenty	**D** much
34	**A** who	**B** what	**C** where	**D** which
35	**A** final	**B** end	**C** limit	**D** finish

42

WRITING

Part 1

Questions 1–5

Here are some sentences about getting a job.
For each question, complete the second sentence so that it means the same as the first.
Use no more than three words.
Write only the missing words on your answer sheet.
You may use this page for any rough work.

Example:

0   There are some advertisements for jobs in the local newspaper.

   The local newspaper .... some advertisements for jobs.

Answer: | 0 | has |

---

1   Filling in a job application form doesn't take you long.

   It doesn't take you long .... in a job application form.

2   At a job interview they will want to know what jobs you have done before.

   At a job interview they will ask, 'What jobs .... before?'

3   It's important to arrive at work on time.

   It's important .... late for work.

4   Some people like working outdoors more than working inside.

   Some people .... working outdoors to working inside.

5   At some firms, staff are given free uniforms.

   Some firms .... their staff free uniforms.

Test 2

Part 2

Question 6

You are going to be absent from your English class next week.

Write a note to your English teacher. In your note, you should

- explain why you are going to be absent
- apologise to your teacher
- ask your teacher for information about next week's work.

Write **35–45 words** on your answer sheet.

Part 3

Write an answer to **one** of the questions (**7** or **8**) in this part.
Write your answer in about **100 words** on your answer sheet.
Tick the box (**Question 7** or **Question 8**) on your answer sheet to show which question you have answered.

Question 7

- This is part of a letter you receive from your new penfriend, Jenna.

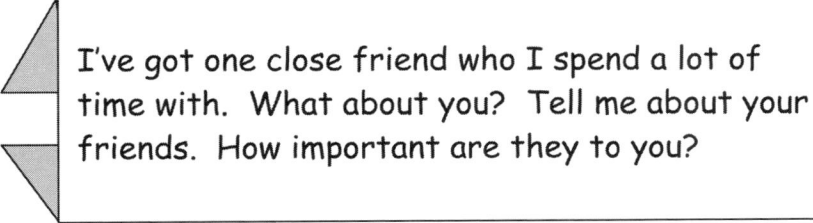

> I've got one close friend who I spend a lot of time with. What about you? Tell me about your friends. How important are they to you?

- Now write a letter to Jenna about your friends.
- Write your **letter** in about 100 words on your answer sheet.

Question 8

- Your English teacher has asked you to write a story.
- Your story must begin with this sentence:

  It was getting dark and I was completely lost.

- Write your **story** in about 100 words on your answer sheet.

Test 2

PAPER 2   LISTENING TEST   approx 35 minutes
(including 6 minutes transfer time)

Part 1

Questions 1–7

There are seven questions in this part.
For each question there are three pictures and a short recording.
Choose the correct picture and put a tick (✓) in the box below it.

Example: How did the woman get to work?

A ✓   B ☐   C ☐

1   What has the boy lost?

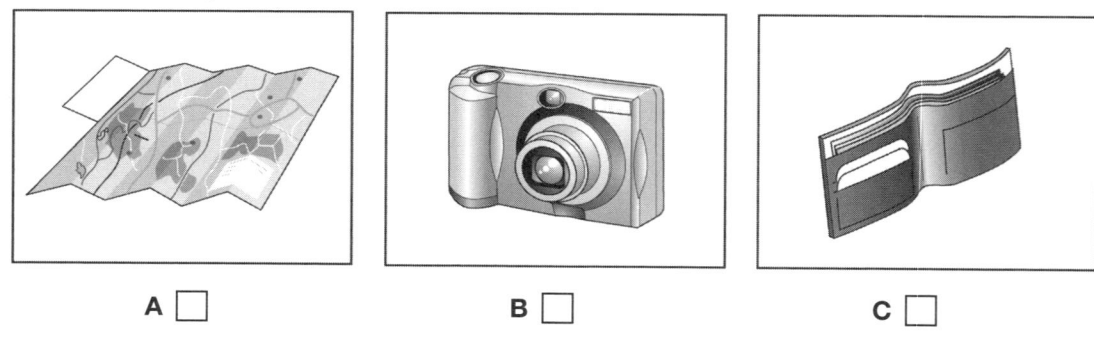

A ☐   B ☐   C ☐

2   What time does the race begin?

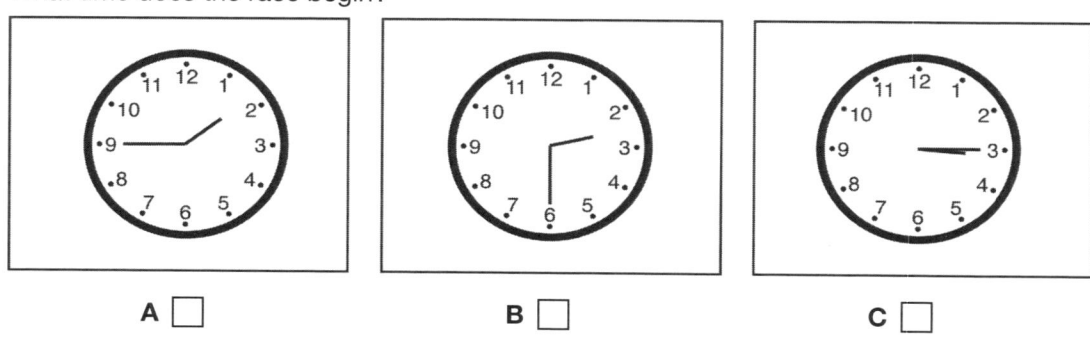

A ☐   B ☐   C ☐

Listening

3 Which musical instrument does the boy play now?

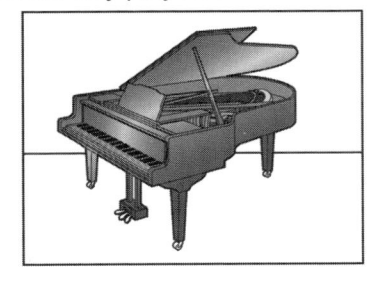

A ☐   B ☐   C ☐

4 What will the weather be like tomorrow afternoon?

A ☐   B ☐   C ☐

5 What is the subject of James Wilson's book?

A ☐   B ☐   C ☐

Test 2

6 Which part of the man's body hurts him at the moment?

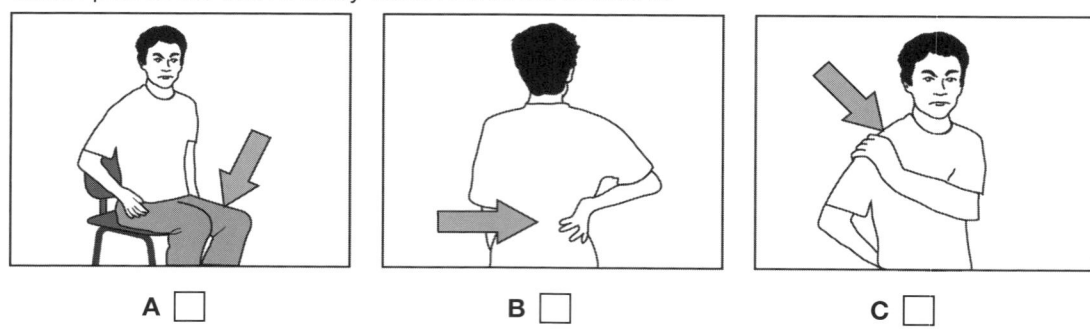

A ☐   B ☐   C ☐

7 Where was the man's knowledge of Spanish useful?

A ☐   B ☐   C ☐

Part 2

Questions 8–13

You will hear a radio interview with a man called Harry Park, who is talking about the adventure travel company he runs.
For each question, put a tick (✓) in the correct box.

8 Harry first became interested in adventure travel because his father
- A ☐ gave him adventure stories to read.
- B ☐ worked in a travel company.
- C ☐ talked a lot about the places he'd been to.

9 Harry decided to start an adventure travel company because he
- A ☐ wanted to share his experience with others.
- B ☐ thought he could make a lot of money.
- C ☐ hoped to do more travelling himself.

10 Who suggested the name for Harry's company?
- A ☐ a friend
- B ☐ a customer
- C ☐ his wife

11 When Harry visits a place, he tries to
- A ☐ give the local people jobs.
- B ☐ take modern equipment.
- C ☐ avoid damaging the area.

Test 2

12 What does Harry say about doing dangerous things?

    A ☐ It's part of his job.
    B ☐ It's frightening.
    C ☐ It's enjoyable.

13 What is Harry's favourite place?

    A ☐ a mountain
    B ☐ a building
    C ☐ a river

Part 3

Questions 14–19

You will hear a man telling some young people about a four-week study programme in a college. For each question, fill in the missing information in the numbered space.

STUDY PROGRAMME

Courses available on:
- English Literature
- 18th century **(14)** ....
- Modern Architecture

Dates for all courses:
- start date: 14th June
- end date: **(15)** ....
- classes: every day except **(16)** ....

Course fees: £425 each

Reduced prices for **(17)** ....

Included in price:
- accommodation and food
- use of the library
- social activities
- books

Not included in price:
- extra **(18)** ....
- transport

Available from college secretary:
- registration forms
- a copy of the **(19)** .... for your course

Test 2

Part 4

Questions 20–25

Look at the six sentences for this part.
You will hear a conversation between a girl, Claire, and a boy, Tom, about a football tour.
Decide if each sentence is correct or incorrect.
If it is correct, put a tick (✓) in the box under **A** for **YES**. If it is not correct, put a tick (✓) in the box under **B** for **NO**.

		A YES	B NO
20	Claire has read about the football tour in a newspaper.	☐	☐
21	Claire is worried about being the youngest member of the team.	☐	☐
22	Tom feels that schoolwork is more important than sports training.	☐	☐
23	Claire intends to study at a university next year.	☐	☐
24	Claire thinks it's important to win every game on the tour.	☐	☐
25	Tom agrees to go and support Claire's team at her next match.	☐	☐

About the Speaking test

The Speaking test lasts about 10 to 12 minutes. You take the test with another candidate. There are two examiners in the room. One examiner talks to you and the other examiner listens to you. Both the examiners give you marks.

Part 1

The examiners introduce themselves and then one examiner asks you and your partner to say your names and spell them. This examiner then asks you questions about yourself, your daily life, interests, etc.

Part 2

The examiner asks you to talk about something together and gives you a drawing to help you.

Part 3

You each have a chance to talk by yourselves. The examiner gives you a colour photograph to look at and asks you to talk about it. When you have finished talking, the examiner gives your partner a different photograph to look at and to talk about.

Part 4

The examiner asks you and your partner to say more about the subject of the photographs in Part 3. You may be asked to give your opinion or to talk about something that has happened to you.

Test 3

PAPER 1　READING AND WRITING TEST　(1 hour 30 minutes)

READING

Part 1

Questions 1–5

Look at the text in each question.
What does it say?
Mark the correct letter **A**, **B** or **C** on your answer sheet.

Example:

0   **NO BICYCLES AGAINST GLASS PLEASE**

A Do not leave your bicycle touching the window.

B Broken glass may damage your bicycle tyres.

C Your bicycle may not be safe here.

Answer: 0 **A** B C

---

1   **THIS DESK IS ONLY FOR THE COLLECTION OF THEATRE TICKETS BOOKED IN ADVANCE**

A You can buy a ticket at this desk to go straight into the theatre.

B You can book theatre tickets in advance at the collection desk.

C You can pick up theatre tickets here that you have already booked.

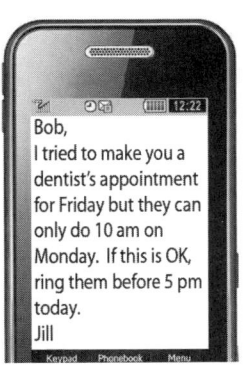

Reading

2

Bob,
I tried to make you a dentist's appointment for Friday but they can only do 10 am on Monday. If this is OK, ring them before 5 pm today.
Jill

Bob needs to

A make a dentist's appointment for Jill.

B phone the dentist about an appointment.

C tell Jill when he can go to the dentist.

3

IF YOUR SHOES ARE DIRTY, PLEASE REMOVE THEM BEFORE ENTERING THIS CHANGING ROOM

A You can keep your shoes on in the changing room unless they are dirty.

B Clean your shoes at the entrance to the changing room before you come in.

C All shoes must be taken off and left at the changing room entrance.

4

MESSAGE

Tony
Maria's sorry but she's going to be late this evening. The train is delayed again! Don't forget you're meeting her at the station. She should be there at 7.15.
Anita

What is Anita doing?

A explaining that she will be late

B apologising for missing the meeting

C reminding somebody of an arrangement

5

INTERNATIONAL STUDENTS' CLUB

Next Saturday's coach trip is cancelled because of lack of interest

A To avoid us cancelling another Saturday trip, tell us what your interests are.

B Saturday's coach trip is cancelled because there are transport problems.

C We are cancelling the trip on Saturday as numbers are too low.

55

Test 3

Part 2

Questions 6–10

The people below all want to do an activity in the countryside during the autumn.
On the opposite page there are descriptions of eight companies which provide leisure activities in the countryside.
Decide which company would be the most suitable for the following people.
For questions **6–10**, mark the correct letter (**A–H**) on your answer sheet.

6 Susanna only has a couple of hours free. She hates walking and would like to try something that brings her into contact with animals, although she is a bit nervous with them.

7 Kemal is looking for some excitement and is keen to do something challenging. He also wants to get to know the area better. He can afford up to £50.

8 Frank and Sabine want to go for a walk with their young family. They'd like to have lunch out but Sabine doesn't like carrying things for the baby, or picnic things, around all day.

9 Charlotte is flying to the Brazilian rainforest soon to do some scientific research. She hopes to get some experience of living in the open air before she goes.

10 Tom wants to explore the natural beauty of the area in company with other people, doing something other than walking. He doesn't have any equipment of his own but he has £40 to spend.

56

Get out this autumn!

A *Windtek*
Windtek runs windsurfing training courses for beginners, involving two three-hour private lessons (£89 with board and wetsuit hire). Experienced surfers can also practise on their own (£15 per hour). At this time of year, the water is still warm and an exciting day in the open air is promised!

B *Country Lanes*
Based in a lovely forest, Country Lanes provides a relaxing experience for newcomers to cycling, experienced cyclists and those just looking for family fun. The one-day group tour (£30 per person) includes bike hire, route map and discounts on entry to tourist attractions.

C *Llama Treks*
For something different, let this company's friendly South American animals accompany you on a walk through the hills. The llamas transport your bags while you enjoy the scenery. The most popular trip is a four-hour walk with a stop at a country restaurant (£55 per adult including meal – children free).

D *Survival School*
If you're thinking of taking a trip to somewhere far from cities and people, you might want to learn how to take care of yourself first. Survival School's challenging weekend course (£150) will teach you fire-making, camp-building and recognising edible plants and wild animals. These skills could save your life.

E *Park Stables*
Have you ever thought of exploring a national park on horseback? Park Stables offers rides on horses specially chosen for their gentle characters. Beginners are welcome and riding hats and boots are provided free of charge. Private ride £25 per hour, family ride £42 per hour.

F *Bygone Age*
Practise a skill from the past! This company owns a 10-kilometre private railway track and offers train-lovers the opportunity to drive a steam train through pretty countryside. The return trip (£125) lasts one hour. There are picnic tables and a children's playground at the station.

G *Swallow Aviation*
Get a bird's-eye view of the countryside and see some of the region's tourist sights from the air by taking a lesson in a two-seater microlight plane. It's an adventure that's not for the faint-hearted! The training plane is an Icarus C42 which flies at around 160 kph. Flights from £49.

H *Island Link*
This ferry company will take you to a beautiful, walker-friendly island. Some of its footpaths take in the coastline, while others pass through woods. You probably won't see another walker all day! Walks vary in length from 2 to 8 hours. Ferry fare and walker's guidebook £5.

Test 3

Part 3

Questions 11–20

Look at the sentences below about two climbers called Gertrude Benham and Charles Fay.
Read the text on the opposite page to decide if each sentence is correct or incorrect.
If it is correct, mark **A** on your answer sheet.
If it is not correct, mark **B** on your answer sheet.

---

11   Gertrude Benham had spent less time climbing in Canada than Charles Fay.

12   Charles Fay applied to an organisation to have a mountain named after him.

13   On 19 July, Gertrude Benham found out she had made a mistake.

14   Gertrude Benham decided to climb Mount Heejee with Charles Fay on 20 July.

15   Charles Fay blamed his guide when he failed to reach the top of Mount Heejee.

16   Gertrude Benham took a different route up Mount Heejee from Charles Fay.

17   Gertrude Benham knew Hans Kaufmann had a plan to choose a slow route up Mount Heejee.

18   The mountain which was named after Charles Fay was the one he had first chosen.

19   Charles Fay's grandson followed a different route from his grandfather up Mount Fay.

20   The hut named after Charles Fay is still used by climbers.

Climbing mountains

Gertrude Benham was born in England in 1867. She had made 130 climbs in the European Alps before going to the Canadian Rocky Mountains in 1904, where she spent the summer climbing. In 1904, the paths of Gertrude Benham and Charles Fay briefly crossed. He had spent several successful summers climbing in the Rocky Mountains. In fact he was so successful that the Geographical Board of Canada asked him to select a mountain to take his name. He chose one known as Heejee and was determined to be the first to reach the top. But Gertrude Benham had the same idea.

On 19 July 1904, Gertrude and her guide, Christian Kaufmann, reached the top of a mountain which they thought was Heejee. Upon their return, however, they were told that that particular mountain was called something else. They decided to try again the next day but, unknown to Gertrude, Charles Fay and his guide Hans Kaufmann, Christian's brother, were planning to climb Heejee that day as well.

Both groups set out on 20 July but Charles Fay and Hans Kaufmann found the snow conditions difficult and had to turn back. Gertrude and Christian were successful. Charles Fay was annoyed and later wrote in a letter, 'Hans Kaufmann led me, against my wishes, up Consolation Valley instead of taking my advice to go round Moraine Lake, while Christian led Miss Benham straight to the top of the mountain.'

Some people said that the Kaufmann brothers had wanted Gertrude to get to the top first and Hans had therefore taken Charles Fay on a route which took more time. Although this is a good story, no documents exist to prove this actually happened and it was never thought that Gertrude had any knowledge of it.

Disappointed, Charles Fay asked if he could choose a different mountain to take his name and chose Mount Shappee, but then found out that Gertrude and Christian had climbed that one as well. At this point Charles Fay agreed to have his name attached to Heejee, as he had originally wanted. He finally climbed to its top on 5 August 1904. Half a century later, his grandson climbed the north-eastern side of the mountain, by then known as Mount Fay. No other climber had ever managed to do this.

Gertrude Benham then travelled to New Zealand and Japan to do more climbing before going home to England, spending time in Australia and India on the way. Charles Fay made many more successful climbs. The first hut built in the Canadian Rockies to shelter climbers was called the Fay Hut. It was built in 1927 but unfortunately was destroyed in a forest fire in 2003.

Part 4

Questions 21–25

Read the text and questions below.
For each question, mark the correct letter **A**, **B**, **C** or **D** on your answer sheet.

At home in Venice
by Francesco da Mosto

I was born in Venice, one of the most popular tourist destinations in Italy, and studied architecture at university here. Though I have also spent time away, I have always come back because it's my home.

In Venice, there are no roads, only canals, so you have to get around on foot or by boat. I live on a canal in the Rialto area in a house that was built in 1588 for the Muti family, who were merchants in the silk trade. In the mid-eighteenth century, it was home to the Vezzi family, who made things like plates and bowls in fine china and became rich sending these around the world. These merchants' houses in Venice are like palaces. Their owners had to have space to show off their goods, but the building also had to be an office, a factory, a store and a home. My house came into our family in 1919, when it was bought by my grandfather. He died before I was born but he was the director of a museum where I often do research on old documents. On some of these, I've seen notes in his handwriting, so, in a strange way, I met him through these documents.

Sadly, the population of Venice has dropped from 120,000 in the 1950s to about 60,000 now. This doesn't include the thousands of tourists who come to visit. I welcome the tourists but unless something is done to stop everyday shops like bakeries and chemists from disappearing, the city will die. I want people who love the city to come here to live and work and give Venice back a life that is not just about tourism.

21   What is the writer's main reason for writing this text?

    A   to persuade more tourists to visit his city
    B   to give readers the history of his home town
    C   to say what he feels about his birthplace
    D   to describe some important moments in his life

Reading

22 The family who first owned the writer's home

    A   used to buy and sell silk.
    B   produced plates and bowls.
    C   were skilled architects.
    D   helped to build the canals.

23 What does the writer say about his grandfather?

    A   His grandfather taught him how to study documents.
    B   He didn't find his grandfather's handwriting easy to read.
    C   He wasn't able to get to know his grandfather personally.
    D   His grandfather turned his home into a museum.

24 What is the writer's attitude to Venice today?

    A   He hopes tourists will stop visiting the city.
    B   He would like people to get jobs working with tourists.
    C   He believes the city would benefit from having fewer inhabitants.
    D   He thinks local businesses should be encouraged to stay.

25 What might the writer say about his house?

A I have never lived anywhere else apart from in my home in the Rialto area of Venice.

B My house is on a canal in Venice and my family, starting with my grandfather, have lived there since 1919.

C We don't know who lived in the house before 1588 but it was owned by merchants from then until the eighteenth century.

D The house was made bigger in the mid-eighteenth century because the owner wanted it to look like a palace.

Test 3

Part 5

Questions 26–35

Read the text below and choose the correct word for each space.
For each question, mark the correct letter **A**, **B**, **C** or **D** on your answer sheet.

Example:

| 0 | **A** over | **B** above | **C** up | **D** ahead |

Answer: 0 **A** ■ B ☐ C ☐ D ☐

Cave Paintings in Australia

A cave containing **(0)** .... 200 paintings was discovered in the Wollemi National Park, Australia, eight years ago. Some of the paintings are **(26)** .... least 3,000 years old. **(27)** .... is even more surprising is that the cave was found by chance by someone walking in the area. However, the site of the cave was so difficult to reach that it **(28)** .... a long time before researchers could visit it.

The exact location of the site has to be **(29)** .... secret. This is to **(30)** .... the cave from being visited by sightseers who do not **(31)** .... how easy it is to **(32)** .... the paintings.

The paintings show people and animals, **(33)** .... birds, lizards and other Australian animals that can **(34)** .... be seen today. According to researchers, **(35)** .... its recent discovery, nobody had visited the cave for around 200 years.

26	**A** in	**B** of	**C** to	**D** at
27	**A** How	**B** What	**C** Why	**D** Which
28	**A** lasted	**B** spent	**C** took	**D** finished
29	**A** remained	**B** set	**C** controlled	**D** kept
30	**A** prevent	**B** miss	**C** escape	**D** avoid
31	**A** catch	**B** realise	**C** dream	**D** feel
32	**A** waste	**B** injure	**C** damage	**D** upset
33	**A** involving	**B** adding	**C** including	**D** consisting
34	**A** yet	**B** already	**C** ever	**D** still
35	**A** by	**B** after	**C** until	**D** on

62

WRITING

Part 1

Questions 1–5

Here are some sentences about sailing.
For each question, complete the second sentence so that it means the same as the first.
Use no more than three words.
Write only the missing words on your answer sheet.
You may use this page for any rough work.

Example:

0 Both my father and I love sailing.

  I love sailing and .... **my father.**

Answer: | 0 | *so does* |

---

1 My father was given his first boat by his parents.

  My father's parents .... **his first boat.**

2 My father doesn't have that boat any more.

  My father .... **got that boat any more.**

3 I wanted to start sailing, but my father insisted that I took some lessons first.

  I wanted to start sailing, but my father said I had .... **some lessons first.**

4 My local sailing school said I was too young to join their courses.

  My local sailing school said I wasn't .... **to join their courses.**

5 I found it more difficult to learn than I had expected.

  It wasn't .... **to learn as I had expected.**

Test 3

Part 2

Question 6

You recently did a homework project about life in Britain, and your penfriend Judy helped you by sending some information.

Write an email to Judy. In your email, you should

- thank her for her help
- explain which information was most useful to you
- say what your teacher thought about your project.

Write **35–45 words** on your answer sheet.

Visual material for the Speaking test

1A

Visual material for the Speaking test

1B

2C

2A

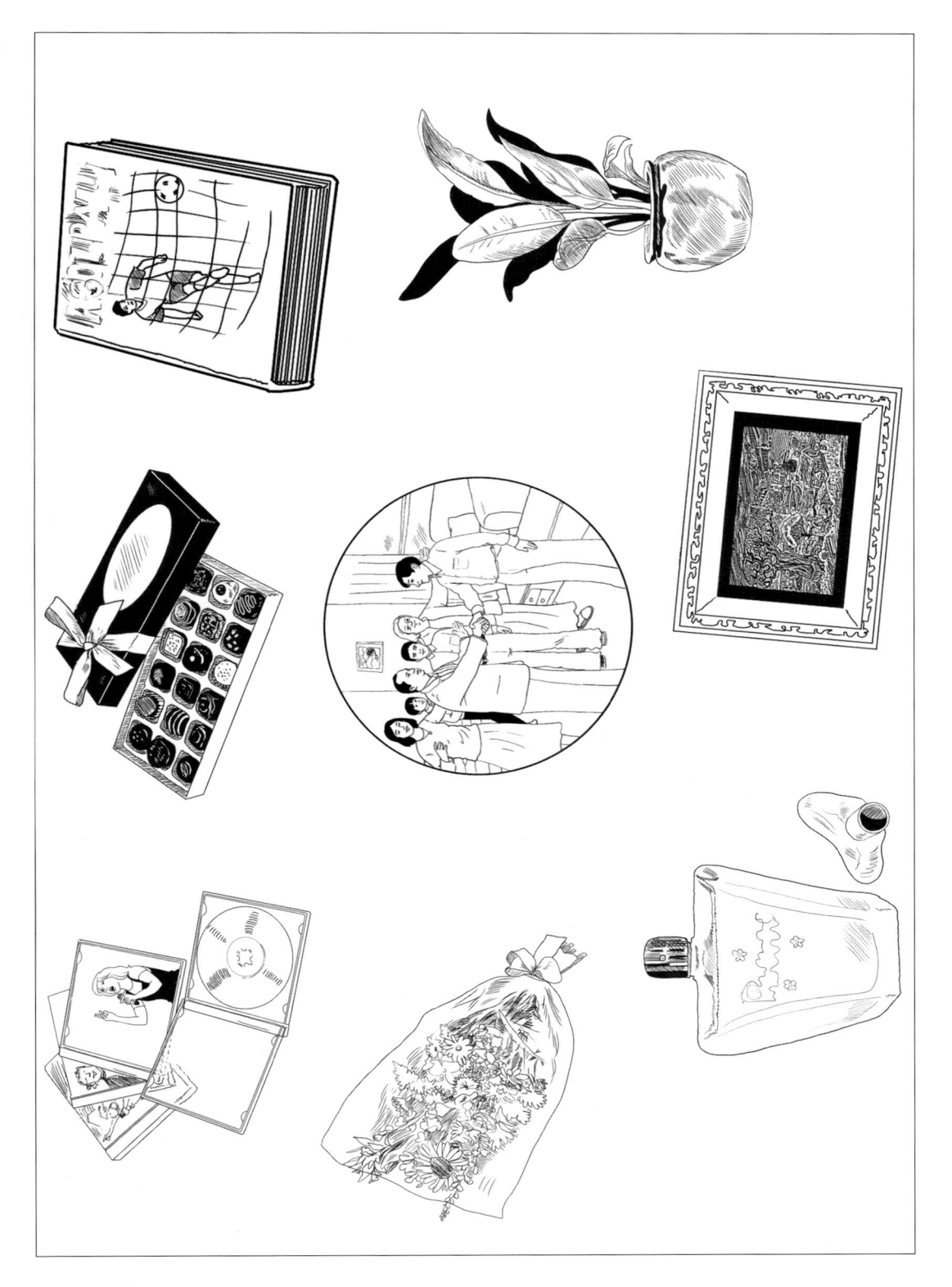

Visual material for the Speaking test

Visual material for the Speaking test

4B

1C

IV

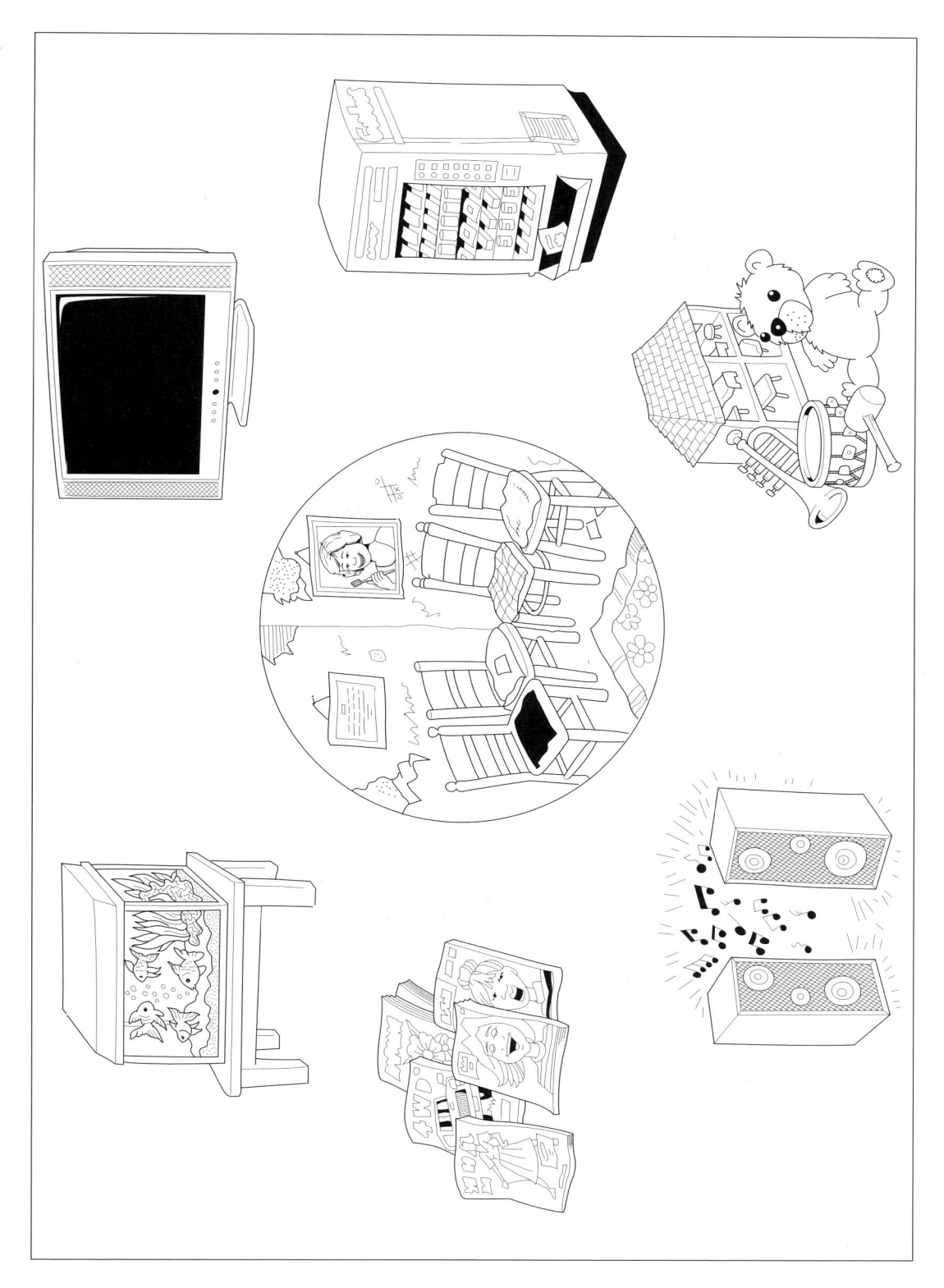

3A

Visual material for the Speaking test

V

Visual material for the Speaking test

3B

4C

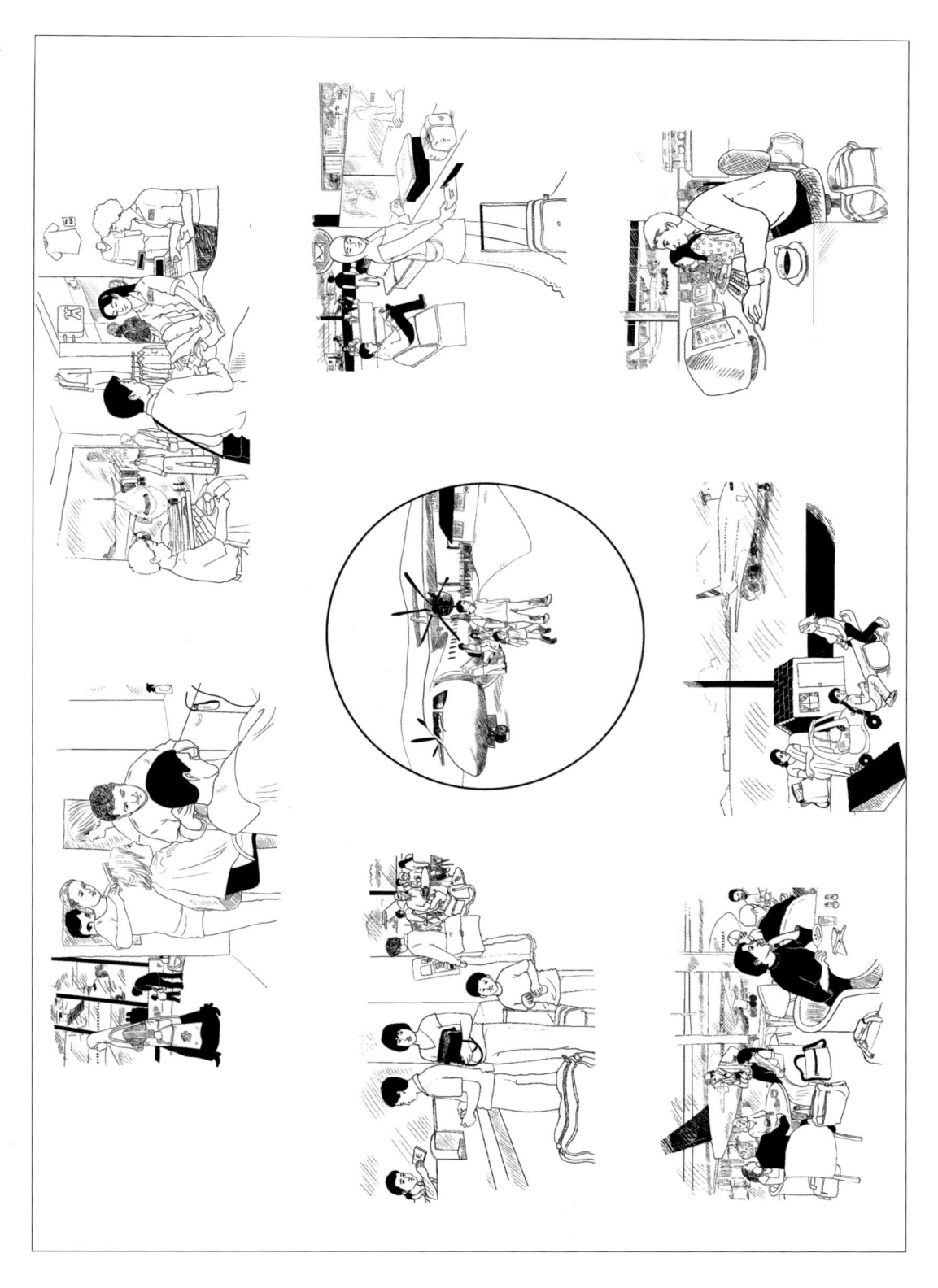

Visual material for the Speaking test

4A

Visual material for the Speaking test

2B

3C

4D

VIII

Part 3

Write an answer to **one** of the questions (**7** or **8**) in this part.
Write your answer in about **100 words** on your answer sheet.
Tick the box (**Question 7** or **Question 8**) on your answer sheet to show which question you have answered.

Question 7

- This is part of a letter you receive from your English friend, Sue.

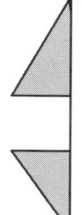

> Tell me about TV in your country. Are the programmes interesting? How much TV do you watch? Do people watch too much TV these days?

- Now write a letter to Sue, answering her questions.
- Write your **letter** in about 100 words on your answer sheet.

Question 8

- Your English teacher wants you to write a story.
- Your story must begin with this sentence:

  I looked in the shop window and I saw exactly what I wanted.

- Write your **story** in about 100 words on your answer sheet.

Test 3

PAPER 2 LISTENING TEST approx 35 minutes
(including 6 minutes transfer time)

Part 1

Questions 1–7

There are seven questions in this part.
For each question there are three pictures and a short recording.
Choose the correct picture and put a tick (✓) in the box below it.

Example: Where did the man leave his camera?

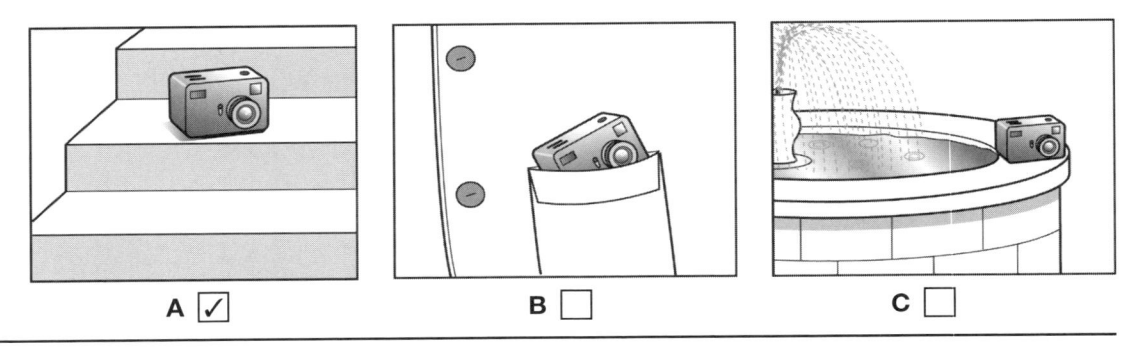

A ✓   B ☐   C ☐

1 Which present will the girl receive?

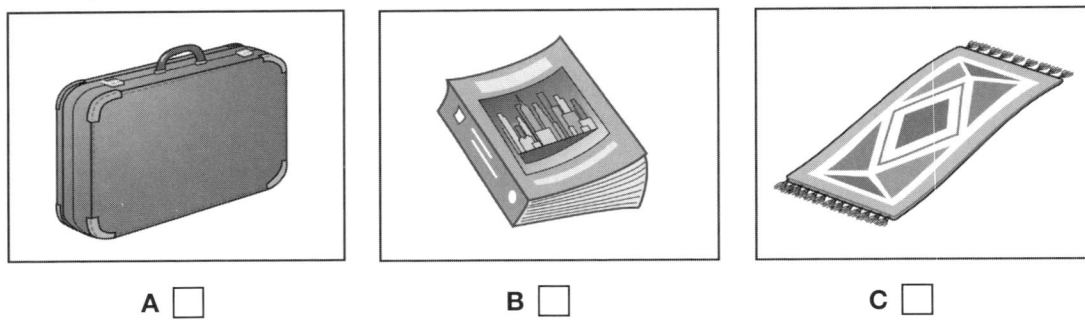

A ☐   B ☐   C ☐

2 Where will the tourists go last?

A ☐   B ☐   C ☐

66

Listening

3 How much does the man pay for the postage?

A ☐ €7.50 B ☐ €15.50 C ☐ €18.50

4 Where in the theatre did the woman leave her gloves?

A ☐ B ☐ C ☐

5 Which dress does the woman like best?

A ☐ B ☐ C ☐

67

Test 3

6 What is the television programme about?

A ☐   **B** ☐   **C** ☐

7 Which vehicle does Steve intend to buy?

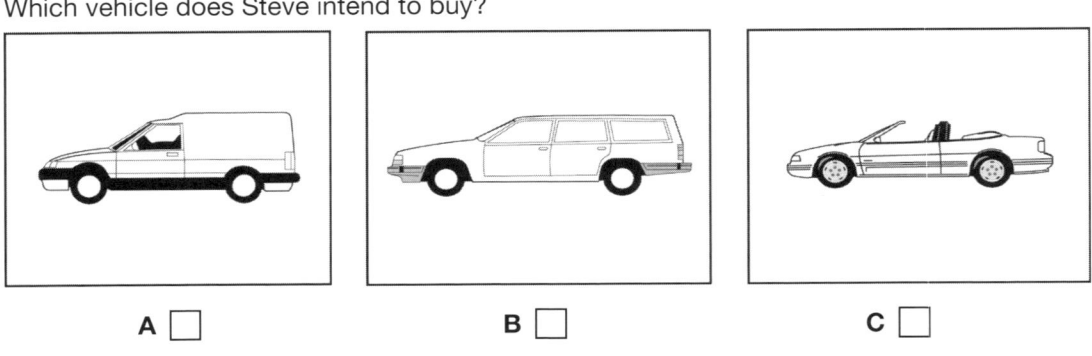

A ☐   **B** ☐   **C** ☐

Part 2

Questions 8–13

You will hear part of a radio interview with a woman called Linda Brown, who is talking about working in a cake shop when she was a student.
For each question, put a tick (✓) in the correct box.

---

8 Linda worked in a cake shop because

- A ☐ her parents didn't give her enough money.
- B ☐ she wanted to give her parents some money.
- C ☐ she needed to buy things for college.

9 Linda liked her first boss because he

- A ☐ paid her well.
- B ☐ was kind to her.
- C ☐ sent her on a training course.

10 What did Linda enjoy about working in the shop?

- A ☐ eating the cakes
- B ☐ the smell of baking
- C ☐ the clean workplace

11 In the shop, Linda helped with

- A ☐ baking bread.
- B ☐ displaying cakes.
- C ☐ making sandwiches.

Test 3

12 Linda says that the full-time shop assistants

A ☐ were friendly to her.
B ☐ hadn't got the same skills as her.
C ☐ didn't work as hard as her.

13 What does Linda say about serving customers?

A ☐ She didn't like dealing with complaints.
B ☐ She liked giving them advice.
C ☐ She enjoyed the busy part of the day.

Part 3

Questions 14–19

You will hear some recorded information about a museum.
For each question, fill in the missing information in the numbered space.

Central Museum

The museum gardens were first created in the year (14) ....

There are exhibitions of English furniture and (15) .... art.

In the museum shop, visitors can buy (16) .... , cards and books.

Cars can be parked at the (17) .... near the museum.

Regular buses to the museum leave from both the city centre and the (18) ....

Call 451858 to find out more about (19) .... visits or room hire.

Test 3

Part 4

Questions 20–25

Look at the six sentences for this part.
You will hear a conversation between a boy, Sam, and a girl, Carla, about a school concert.
Decide if each sentence is correct or incorrect.
If it is correct, put a tick (✓) in the box under **A** for **YES**. If it is not correct, put a tick (✓) in the box under **B** for **NO**.

		A YES	B NO
20	Carla is surprised that Mrs Ford wanted her to attend the meeting.	☐	☐
21	Sam says that last year's concert was an improvement on earlier ones.	☐	☐
22	Carla enjoyed preparing for last year's concert.	☐	☐
23	Sam tells Carla that she is the best pianist in the school.	☐	☐
24	Sam encourages Carla to accept Mrs Ford's choice of music.	☐	☐
25	Sam realises that he must stop doing one of his activities.	☐	☐

About the Speaking test

The Speaking test lasts about 10 to 12 minutes. You take the test with another candidate. There are two examiners in the room. One examiner talks to you and the other examiner listens to you. Both the examiners give you marks.

Part 1

The examiners introduce themselves and then one examiner asks you and your partner to say your names and spell them. This examiner then asks you questions about yourself, your daily life, interests, etc.

Part 2

The examiner asks you to talk about something together and gives you a drawing to help you.

Part 3

You each have a chance to talk by yourselves. The examiner gives you a colour photograph to look at and asks you to talk about it. When you have finished talking, the examiner gives your partner a different photograph to look at and to talk about.

Part 4

The examiner asks you and your partner to say more about the subject of the photographs in Part 3. You may be asked to give your opinion or to talk about something that has happened to you.

Test 4

PAPER 1   READING AND WRITING TEST   (1 hour 30 minutes)

READING

Part 1

Questions 1–5

Look at the text in each question.
What does it say?
Mark the correct letter **A**, **B** or **C** on your answer sheet.

Example:

0

> Jake
>
> Ben left his bike in our garage yesterday. He'd like to come and collect it at 6. Please be at home to let him into the garage.
>
> Sonia

What does Jake need to do?

A open the garage when Ben arrives so he can get his bike

B look in the garage and let Ben know if his bike is there

C get Ben's bike out of the garage and take it to him

Answer: 0 **A** B C

1

> ✶**End of Term Party**✶
> December 15th 7–10 pm
> Sign below if you can come!
> We also need people to
> help organise the event –
> call Sophie (678853)

A You need to phone Sophie if you want to come to this event.

B Anyone wanting to take part in running this event should sign the notice.

C People who can attend this event should put their names on the notice.

74

Reading

2

> New Message
> From: Hintonexhibitions@TCK.co.uk
> Subject: Guitar Show
>
> The Guitar Show returns to Hinton Exhibition Centre on 6 March. Many new guitars will be on display. The show is open to schools and the general public.

The main purpose of this email is

A to invite people to display goods at an exhibition.

B to explain booking details for a show.

C to provide information about an event.

3

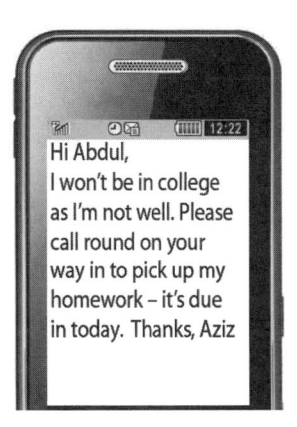

> Hi Abdul,
> I won't be in college as I'm not well. Please call round on your way in to pick up my homework – it's due in today. Thanks, Aziz

Aziz wants Abdul to

A take his homework to college for him.

B call their college to say that he is not well.

C pick up any new homework given out at college today.

4

> Once opened, remove any unused soup from the tin and place in the refrigerator.
>
> SOUP

This label gives advice on

A how to store the product.

B how to use the product.

C how to open the product.

5

> **Wanted: Kitchen Assistants**
>
> Evenings or weekends
> Free meals
> Full training provided
> Apply inside

A Only people who are trained in kitchen work should apply for these part-time jobs.

B There are part-time opportunities for people without experience of working in a kitchen.

C We offer cheap meals to people who work part-time in our kitchen.

Test 4

Part 2

Questions 6–10

The people below all want to visit a museum.
On the opposite page there are descriptions of eight museums.
Decide which museum would be the most suitable for the following people.
For questions **6–10**, mark the correct letter (**A–H**) on your answer sheet.

6   Jake and Maureen have different interests but want to go somewhere they will both enjoy. Jake loves anything to do with the sea, while Maureen's interested in social history and the lives of women.

7   Melanie is a history teacher. She wants to take her class to a museum where they will be allowed to touch things and have activities to do during their visit.

8   Roger is keen to find out about different forms of transport in towns over the last hundred years. He would like to attend a talk while he is at the museum.

9   Kazuko studies English literature and thinks that seeing where writers lived will help her understand their books better. She finds it useful to look at pictures which are connected with the books.

10   Nick is more interested in learning about the countryside than learning about people from the past. He needs information for some schoolwork he is doing about what happens to rivers and hills over time.

Recommended Museums in the Area

A Red House
Travel back to the time of the novelist Charlotte Brontë and find out about her friends and local connections. Discover the comforts and discomforts of the 1830s country home where Charlotte sometimes stayed as a guest of Joshua Taylor's family and got ideas for her novel *Shirley*.

B Castle Museum
The castle was built looking down on the valley of the River Dean. It is now a museum, where you can learn how the valley has changed over millions of years. There is a collection of interesting rocks and fossils found in the area, and pictures showing how the valley probably looked in prehistoric times.

C Hillcrest Museum
Enjoy an experience of digging up the past. Handle pieces of ancient pots, tools and other objects from many countries. Learn to date them and see what they tell us about how people lived then. Also try out computer programs which help plan the digging-up of sites. School groups should book in advance.

D Shandy Hall
Here in the 1760s, Laurence Sterne wrote *Tristram Shandy*. His fifteenth-century house is now surrounded by a large garden full of beautiful and unusual plants. Inside there is an important collection of Sterne's novels plus the original drawings which were included in his works.

E Museum of Peace
Situated in beautiful countryside, this is the only museum of its kind in the country. It has a growing collection of art and objects connected with peace history, non-violence and the ending of war. It also has material which can be used after the visit back in the classroom.

F Fishing Centre
Study the routes used by fishermen over the last two hundred years and see how their ocean-going boats worked. A new exhibition explores the position of wives and mothers in the old fishing towns, giving information about their occupations, and their attitudes to work and home.

G Viking Centre
Come and experience what life was like 1,200 years ago in this Viking town, rebuilt at the mouth of the river. Our introductory talk will inform you about the close relationship the Vikings had with the sea – they were excellent fishermen, sailors and boat-builders. There are also tools, clothes and everyday items to look at.

H Horsepower Museum
This museum reminds us just how important horses were to life in the nineteenth and early twentieth centuries. It has a permanent exhibition of old trams and buses, which used to be pulled through the streets by horses. The staff here are very knowledgeable and give daily lectures on this fascinating collection

Test 4

Part 3

Questions 11–20

Look at the sentences below about John Chapman, an Englishman who lived in the 15th century.
Read the text on the opposite page to decide if each sentence is correct or incorrect.
If it is correct, mark **A** on your answer sheet.
If it is not correct, mark **B** on your answer sheet.

---

11   In 1440, John Chapman lived in Norwich.

12   John rarely managed to sell all his goods at the market.

13   John and his wife had enough money to live comfortably.

14   John's wife encouraged him to make the journey to London.

15   People stopped to chat to John while he was standing on London Bridge.

16   John was disappointed by what the old man told him.

17   John's wife realised why he was digging a hole under the tree.

18   The writing on the box was in a language that was foreign to John.

19   The second container was buried directly under the first.

20   The people of Swaffham benefitted from John's good luck.

John Chapman

The atmosphere in the market place in Norwich in 1440 was probably not very different from how it is today – noisy, crowded, colourful and exciting. It was here that John Chapman used to come each week from his home in Swaffham, 50 kilometres away, to try to sell his copper pots and pans.

After one particularly tiring day, he loaded his unsold pots and pans onto the back of his horse as usual and walked slowly home. He had a meal and went to bed, complaining bitterly to his wife about their lack of money. However, that night John had a dream that would change the rest of his life.

In this dream a man told John that if he stood on London Bridge he would hear something that would make him rich. The dream was so real that John couldn't get it out of his mind, and finally he decided to make the journey, even though his wife was against the idea.

After a week's preparation, John set off for London with just his dog for company. When he arrived at London Bridge he stopped and watched all the men and women who went past. Many of them talked to him, but he heard nothing that would make him rich.

On the third day, however, an old man asked him why he was standing there. John told him it was because of a dream. The old man replied, 'I recently dreamed that I went to the home of John Chapman, in Swaffham, and dug under a tree at the back of his house, where I found a buried pot of gold! But I am not foolish enough to believe in dreams.'

Unable to believe his luck, John said goodbye and returned to Swaffham. As soon as he got home, he fetched a spade and started digging. His wife looked on in amazement, unable to understand what he was doing. But sure enough, he uncovered a box. Opening it with nervous hands he found that it was full of money. The couple were delighted, but also curious about some words on the lid, which were in a language they didn't recognise. Keen to find out their meaning, John put the box in his window and soon two young men knocked on the door and translated them for him: *Beneath me lies another one much richer*. So John dug deeper and this time found a huge pot full of gold and jewels!

That is how John Chapman became rich. He spent the money wisely and paid for several public buildings to be built. And his memory lives on in Swaffham today, on the painted sign at the entrance to the town!

Part 4

Questions 21–25

Read the text and questions below.
For each question, mark the correct letter **A**, **B**, **C** or **D** on your answer sheet.

Anna Gomez

Anna Gomez is a successful TV sports presenter, but most people still think of her as the famous women's ice-skating champion who won several important competitions when she was younger. 'As a child, my dream was actually to become a ballet dancer – I didn't own any skates until I was nine, and didn't become really keen on skating until I was fourteen,' says Anna. She went on to university where, despite ice-skating almost all the time, she left with an excellent degree. 'I felt I owed it to my parents. They supported me through university, and expected me to do well there – I didn't feel I could disappoint them.'

In a sport where most stars become famous as teenagers, Anna was unusual in being in her twenties before she won any major titles. 'When I was younger, I got very angry at competitions, shouting at judges if I disagreed with them. That made me unpopular, especially with other skaters. My technique was just as good as theirs and I had a very encouraging coach at the time. The problem was in my head – I just didn't think I had what it takes to be a champion. That changed as I won more competitions, and I was performing at my best by the age of twenty-five.'

Anna retired from professional ice-skating five years later, having achieved great success during that period. 'It was a difficult decision. As you get near the end of your career, people always ask when you're going to stop. At the time, I wasn't sure that I was actually ready to give up. But, looking back, I'm glad I stopped when I did. You shouldn't think too much about the past – just move on to the next thing.'

---

21 What is the writer doing in the text?

- **A** discussing the influence of Anna's early life on her career
- **B** giving Anna's reasons for choosing to become a TV presenter
- **C** describing the progress of Anna's professional life in sport
- **D** explaining why Anna was such a successful ice-skater

Reading

22 What do we learn about Anna's time at university?

- **A** Her parents expected her to do better in her studies.
- **B** She spent too much time ice-skating.
- **C** She managed to get good results.
- **D** Her parents wanted her to keep up her ice-skating.

23 Why does Anna believe she failed to win competitions as a teenager?

- **A** She annoyed too many people.
- **B** She was not confident enough in her ability.
- **C** She needed to improve her technique.
- **D** She did not have the right coach.

24 What does Anna say about her retirement from skating?

- **A** She has no regrets about giving up when she did.
- **B** She had wanted to stop for a long time.
- **C** She was persuaded by others that she should retire.
- **D** She missed some things about her life as an ice-skater.

25 Which of the following appeared on a website about Anna?

A Anna Gomez, 20, achieves her life-long ambition of becoming the national women's ice-skating champion.

B TV presenter and former sportswoman Anna Gomez announces her return to professional ice-skating after five years.

C Teenage star Anna Gomez wins another top title, and thanks her many friends in the ice-skating world.

D After five years at the top, ice-skating star Anna Gomez retires and takes up a new job in television.

Test 4

Part 5

Questions 26–35

Read the text below and choose the correct word for each space.
For each question, mark the correct letter **A**, **B**, **C** or **D** on your answer sheet.

Example:

0   **A** known   **B** named   **C** called   **D** thought

Answer: 0 **A** ■ B ☐ C ☐ D ☐

The Driest Place on Earth

The Atacama Desert in Chile is **(0)** .... as the driest place on Earth. It is almost 1,000 kilometres **(26)** .... length, lying between the Pacific Ocean and the Andes mountains. Under a centimetre of rain **(27)** .... annually, and the centre is so dry **(28)** .... scientists have never recorded **(29)** .... rain there.

Over a million people **(30)** .... live in the Atacama today. Most live on the coast, which is also home to teams of astronomers who are there to **(31)** .... advantage of the clear skies. In the north, farmers grow tomatoes with water they have collected from underground rocks. However, for **(32)** .... who have their farms on higher ground, the water comes from melting snow.

People generally seem to **(33)** .... knowledge about what the desert has to offer, but in **(34)** ...., there is plenty to do – from seeing the amazing natural sights to playing golf, one of the more recent activities **(35)** .... tourists to the region.

26	**A** by	**B** at	**C** to	**D** in
27	**A** pours	**B** falls	**C** sinks	**D** lowers
28	**A** as	**B** that	**C** when	**D** than
29	**A** any	**B** no	**C** some	**D** little
30	**A** totally	**B** exactly	**C** actually	**D** finally
31	**A** have	**B** make	**C** get	**D** take
32	**A** those	**B** these	**C** them	**D** they
33	**A** fail	**B** lose	**C** miss	**D** lack
34	**A** case	**B** turn	**C** fact	**D** time
35	**A** arriving	**B** attracting	**C** approaching	**D** arranging

82

WRITING

Part 1

Questions 1–5

Here are some sentences about a trip to the city of Florence in Italy.
For each question, complete the second sentence so that it means the same as the first.
Use no more than three words.
Write only the missing words on your answer sheet.
You may use this page for any rough work.

Example:

0   This will be my first visit to Florence.

   I've .... to Florence before.

Answer: | 0 | never been |

---

1   Florence is not as crowded in winter as it is in summer.

   Florence is .... crowded in winter than in summer.

2   John suggested taking a taxi to the hotel.

   John said, 'If I were you, ... take a taxi to the hotel.'

3   Florence is a very easy city to walk around.

   It is not very .... to walk around Florence.

4   A city like Florence can teach you a lot.

   You can .... a lot in a city like Florence.

5   I will probably visit some museums while I'm in Florence.

   I will probably visit some museums .... my stay in Florence.

Test 4

Part 2

Question 6

You have just bought some new clothes.
Write an email to your friend, Alex. In your email, you should

- tell Alex what clothes you have bought
- say where you bought the clothes from
- explain why you needed to buy these clothes.

Write **35–45 words** on your answer sheet.

Part 3

Write an answer to **one** of the questions (**7** or **8**) in this part.
Write your answer in about **100 words** on your answer sheet.
Tick the box (**Question 7** or **Question 8**) on your answer sheet to show which question you have answered.

Question 7

- This is part of a letter you receive from your English penfriend.

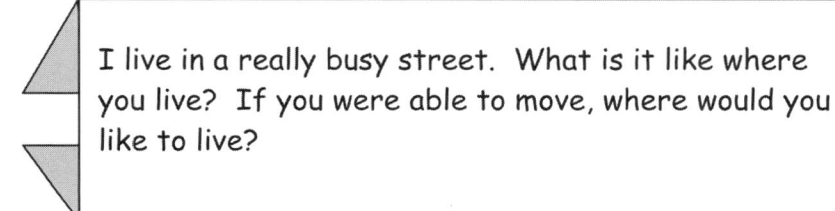

> I live in a really busy street. What is it like where you live? If you were able to move, where would you like to live?

- Now write a letter, answering your penfriend's questions.
- Write your **letter** in about 100 words on your answer sheet.

Question 8

- Your English teacher has asked you to write a story.
- This is the title for your story:

An unusual request

- Write your **story** in about 100 words on your answer sheet.

Test 4

PAPER 2 LISTENING TEST approx 35 minutes
(including 6 minutes transfer time)

Part 1

Questions 1–7

There are seven questions in this part.
For each question there are three pictures and a short recording.
Choose the correct picture and put a tick (✓) in the box below it.

Example: Where did the man leave his camera?

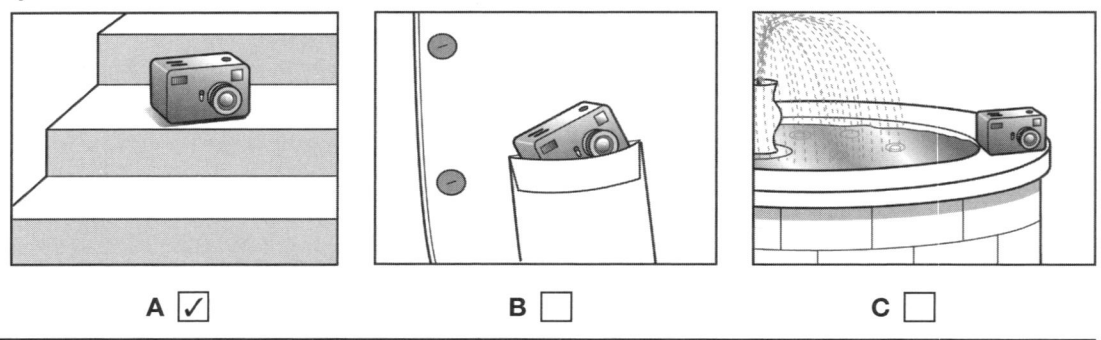

A ✓ B ☐ C ☐

1 Which prize has the man just won?

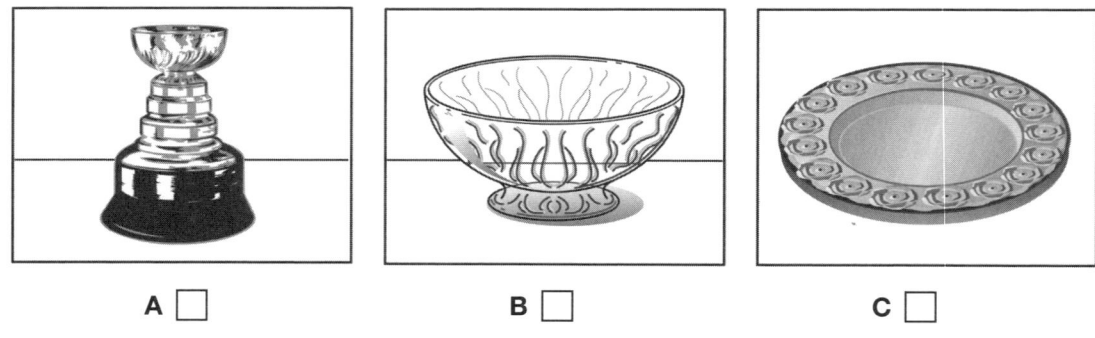

A ☐ B ☐ C ☐

2 What was the man's first job?

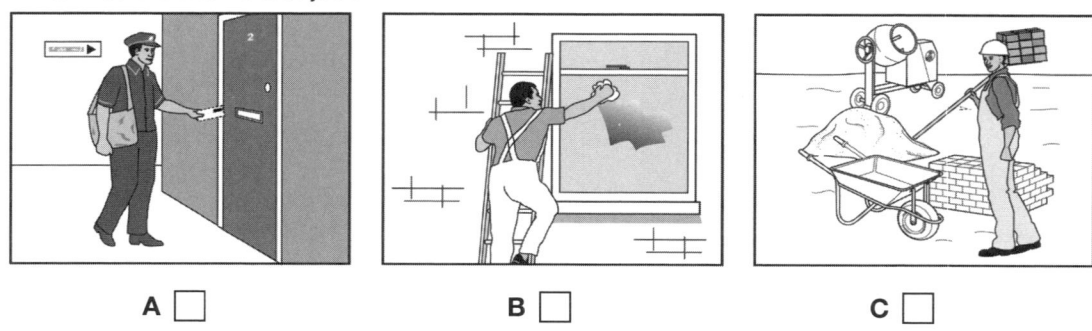

A ☐ B ☐ C ☐

86

Listening

3 Where will they have something to eat?

A ☐ B ☐ C ☐

4 What does the woman's house look like now?

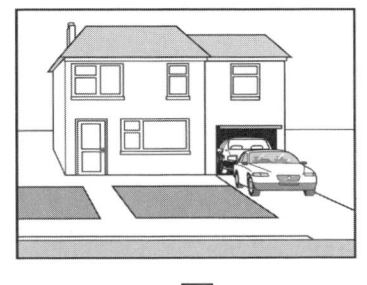

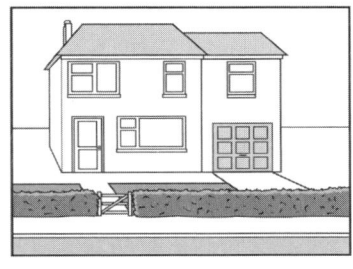

A ☐ B ☐ C ☐

5 Which sport will they do tomorrow?

A ☐ B ☐ C ☐

Test 4

6 What can you see on the television programme?

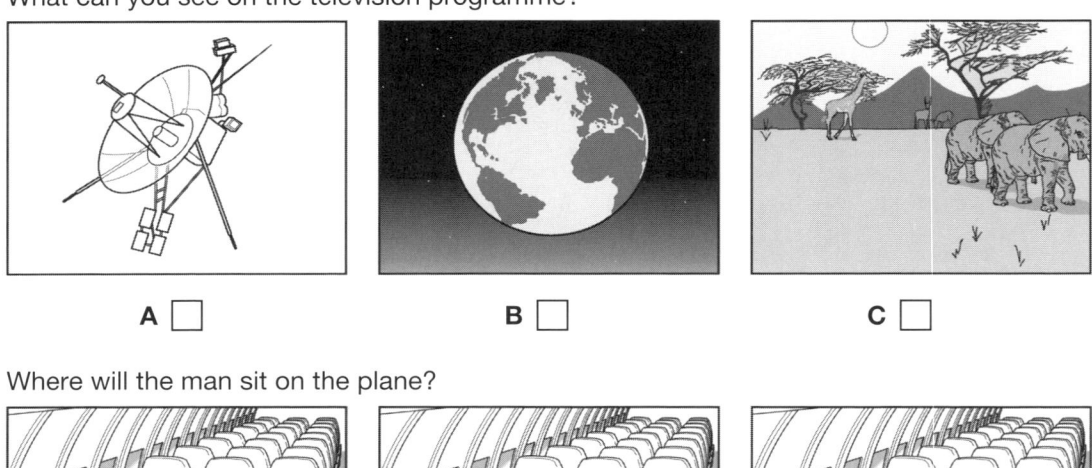

A ☐   B ☐   C ☐

7 Where will the man sit on the plane?

A ☐   B ☐   C ☐

Part 2

Questions 8–13

You will hear an interview with a woman called Lucy Rainbow, who is talking about her job as a painter.
For each question, put a tick (✓) in the correct box.

8   What does Lucy usually paint?

   A ☐ scenery for stage plays
   B ☐ pictures of pop stars
   C ☐ the walls in people's homes

9   Lucy chose her present job because

   A ☐ she enjoys working by herself.
   B ☐ she couldn't get a job in advertising.
   C ☐ she thought it would be interesting.

10   What does Lucy find difficult about her work?

   A ☐ She sometimes misses lunch.
   B ☐ Some days are too busy.
   C ☐ She always has too much work to do.

11   How many hours a day does Lucy usually work?

   A ☐ seven
   B ☐ eight
   C ☐ eleven

Test 4

12 How does Lucy travel to work?

A ☐ on foot
B ☐ by car
C ☐ by public transport

13 What does Lucy do in her free time nowadays?

A ☐ She studies.
B ☐ She visits an art gallery.
C ☐ She plays tennis.

Part 3

Questions 14–19

You will hear a radio announcement about a new magazine.
For each question, fill in the missing information in the numbered space.

NEW MAGAZINE

The name of the magazine is **(14)** ....

First issue of magazine

- healthy recipes using **(15)** ....
- a DVD about making **(16)** .... for summer

Second issue of magazine

- recipes using **(17)** .... for children
- special recipes to use for **(18)** .... for adults

The first issue of the magazine costs **(19)** £ ....

Test 4

Part 4

Questions 20–25

Look at the six sentences for this part.
You will hear a man called Karl, and his wife Jenny, talking about the holiday they have just had.
Decide if each sentence is correct or incorrect.
If it is correct, put a tick (✓) in the box under **A** for **YES**. If it is not correct, put a tick (✓) in the box under **B** for **NO**.

		A YES	B NO
20	Jenny and Karl are both pleased to be home after their holiday.	☐	☐
21	Jenny thinks the weather forecast they heard for their holiday week was correct.	☐	☐
22	Jenny and Karl both liked the way their hotel served meals.	☐	☐
23	Jenny thinks they had a better room on this holiday than last year.	☐	☐
24	Karl was angry about the state of the hotel sports equipment.	☐	☐
25	Jenny and Karl are both keen to plan another holiday immediately.	☐	☐

About the Speaking test

The Speaking test lasts about 10 to 12 minutes. You take the test with another candidate. There are two examiners in the room. One examiner talks to you and the other examiner listens to you. Both the examiners give you marks.

Part 1

The examiners introduce themselves and then one examiner asks you and your partner to say your names and spell them. This examiner then asks you questions about yourself, your daily life, interests, etc.

Part 2

The examiner asks you to talk about something together and gives you a drawing to help you.

Part 3

You each have a chance to talk by yourselves. The examiner gives you a colour photograph to look at and asks you to talk about it. When you have finished talking, the examiner gives your partner a different photograph to look at and to talk about.

Part 4

The examiner asks you and your partner to say more about the subject of the photographs in Part 3. You may be asked to give your opinion or to talk about something that has happened to you.

Frames for the Speaking test

TEST 1

Part 1 (2–3 minutes)

Tasks Identifying oneself; giving information about oneself; talking about interests.

Phase 1
Examiner

A/B Good morning / afternoon / evening.
Can I have your mark sheets, please?

A/B I'm .... and this is ....
He / she is just going to listen to us.

A Now, what's your name?
Thank you.

B And what's your name?
Thank you.

Back-up prompts

B Candidate B, what's your surname?
How do you spell it?

Thank you.

A And, Candidate A, what's your surname?
How do you spell it?

Thank you.

How do you write your family / second name?

How do you write your family / second name?

(Ask the following questions. Use candidates' names throughout. Ask Candidate A first.)

Where do you live / come from?

<u>Adult students</u>
Do you work or are you a student in . . .?
What do you do / study?

<u>School-age students</u>
Do you study English at school?
Do you like it?

Thank you.

(Repeat for Candidate B.)

Do you live in . . .?

Have you got a job?
What job do you do? / What subject(s) do you study?

Do you have English lessons?

Test 1

Phase 2
Examiner

(Select one or more questions from the list to ask each candidate. Ask Candidate B first.)

	Back-up prompts
Do you enjoy studying English? Why (not)?	Do you like studying English?
Do you think that English will be useful for you in the future?	Will you use English in the future?
What did you do yesterday evening / last weekend?	Did you do anything yesterday evening / last weekend? What?
What do you enjoy doing in your free time?	What do you like to do in your free time?

Thank you.

(Introduction to Part 2)

In the next part, you are going to talk to each other.

Part 2 (2–3 minutes)

THROWING THINGS AWAY

Tasks Discussing alternatives; expressing opinions; making choices.

Examiner *Say to both candidates:*

> I'm going to describe a situation to you.
>
> A young man is leaving home to study in another town. His parents want him to throw away some of his things before he goes. Talk together about which things he should keep and which he should throw away.
>
> Here is a picture with some ideas to help you.

Ask both candidates to look at picture 1A on page I of the Student's Book and repeat the frame.

> I'll say that again.
>
> A young man is leaving home to study in another town. His parents want him to throw away some of his things before he goes. Talk together about which things he should keep and which he should throw away.
>
> All right? Talk together.

Allow the candidates enough time to complete the task without intervention. Prompt only if necessary.

95

Frames for the Speaking test

Part 3 (3 minutes)

PEOPLE AT LUNCHTIME

Tasks   Describing people and places; saying where people and things are and what different people are doing.

Examiner   *Say to both candidates:*

> Now, I'd like each of you to talk on your own about something. I'm going to give each of you a photograph of people at lunchtime.
>
> Candidate A, here is your photograph. *(Ask Candidate A to look at photo 1B on page II of the Student's Book.)* Please show it to Candidate B, but I'd like you to talk about it. Candidate B, you just listen. I'll give you your photograph in a moment.
>
> Candidate A, please tell us what you can see in the photograph.

(Candidate A)   *Approximately one minute*

IIf there is a need to intervene, prompts rather than direct questions should be used.

Ask Candidate A to close his/her book.

Examiner

> Now, Candidate B, here is your photograph. It also shows people at lunchtime. *(Ask Candidate B to look at photo IC on page IV of the Student's Book.)* Please show it to Candidate A and tell us what you can see in the photograph.

(Candidate B)   *Approximately one minute*

Ask the candidates to close their books before moving to Part 4.

Part 4 (3 minutes)

Tasks   Talking about one's likes and dislikes; expressing opinions.

Examiner   *Say to both candidates:*

> Your photographs showed people at lunchtime. Now, I'd like you to talk together about what you usually do at lunchtime, during the week and at the weekend.

Allow the candidates enough time to complete the task without intervention. Prompt only if necessary.

Back-up prompts
1. Talk about what **you** do at lunchtime during the **week**.
2. Talk about lunchtime at the **weekend**.
3. Talk about what you **don't like** doing at lunchtime.
4. Talk about why lunch is **important**.

> Thank you. That's the end of the test.

TEST 2

Part 1 (2–3 minutes)

Tasks   Identifying oneself; giving information about oneself; talking about interests.

Phase 1
Examiner

A/B   Good morning / afternoon / evening.
Can I have your mark sheets, please?

A/B   I'm ………… and this is ………… .
He / she is just going to listen to us.

A   Now, what's your name?
Thank you.

B   And what's your name?
Thank you.

Back-up prompts

B   Candidate B, what's your surname?
How do you spell it?

Thank you.

How do you write your family / second name?

A   And, Candidate A, what's your surname?
How do you spell it?

Thank you.

How do you write your family / second name?

(Ask the following questions. Use candidates' names throughout. Ask Candidate A first.)

Where do you live / come from?

Do you live in . . .?

Adult students
Do you work or are you a student in . . .?
What do you do / study?

Have you got a job?
What job do you do? / What subject(s) do you study?

School-age students
Do you study English at school?
Do you like it?

Do you have English lessons?

Thank you.

(Repeat for Candidate B.)

97

Frames for the Speaking test

Phase 2
Examiner

(Select one or more questions from the list to ask each candidate. Ask Candidate B first.)

	Back-up prompts
Do you enjoy studying English? Why (not)?	Do you like studying English?
Do you think that English will be useful for you in the future?	Will you use English in the future?
What did you do yesterday evening / last weekend?	Did you do anything yesterday evening / last weekend? What?
What do you enjoy doing in your free time?	What do you like to do in your free time?

Thank you.

(Introduction to Part 2)

In the next part, you are going to talk to each other.

Part 2 (2–3 minutes)

PRESENT FOR A FRIEND'S FAMILY

Tasks Discussing alternatives; expressing opinions; making choices.

Examiner *Say to both candidates:*

> I'm going to describe a situation to you.
>
> A young man has been invited to stay with a friend's family for a few days. He hasn't met them before and would like to take them a present. Talk together about the different presents he could take and say which would be best for all the family.
>
> Here is a picture with some ideas to help you.

Ask both candidates to look at picture 2A on page III of the Student's Book and repeat the frame.

> I'll say that again.
>
> A young man has been invited to stay with a friend's family for a few days. He hasn't met them before and would like to take them a present. Talk together about the different presents he could take and say which would be best for all the family.
>
> All right? Talk together.

Allow the candidates enough time to complete the task without intervention. Prompt only if necessary.

Part 3 (3 minutes)

TAKING PHOTOS

Tasks Describing people and places; saying where people and things are and what different people are doing.

Examiner *Say to both candidates:*

> Now, I'd like each of you to talk on your own about something. I'm going to give each of you a picture of people taking photos.
>
> Candidate A, here is your picture. (*Ask Candidate A to look at photo 2B on page VIII of the Student's Book.*) Please show it to Candidate B, but I'd like you to talk about it. Candidate B, you just listen. I'll give you your picture in a moment.
>
> Candidate A, please tell us what you can see in the picture.

(Candidate A) *Approximately one minute*

If there is a need to intervene, prompts rather than direct questions should be used.

Ask Candidate A to close his/her book.

Examiner
> Now, Candidate B, here is your picture. It also shows someone taking a photo. (*Ask Candidate B to look at photo 2C on page II of the Student's Book.*) Please show it to Candidate A and tell us what you can see in the picture.

(Candidate B) *Approximately one minute*

Ask the candidates to close their books before moving to Part 4.

Part 4 (3 minutes)

Tasks Talking about one's likes and dislikes; expressing opinions.

Examiner *Say to both candidates:*

> Your pictures showed people taking photos. Now, I'd like you to talk together about the things you like to take photos of and say when you like to take them.

Allow the candidates enough time to complete the task without intervention. Prompt only if necessary.

> **Back-up prompts**
> 1. Talk about the **things / people** you like to take photos of.
> 2. Talk about **when** you like to take photos.
> 3. Talk about what you **do** with your photos.
> 4. Talk about how you **feel** when other people take photos.

> Thank you. That's the end of the test.

Frames for the Speaking test

TEST 3

Part 1 (2–3 minutes)

Tasks Identifying oneself; giving information about oneself; talking about interests.

Phase 1
Examiner

A/B Good morning / afternoon / evening.
Can I have your mark sheets, please?

A/B I'm .... and this is ....
He / she is just going to listen to us.

A Now, what's your name?
Thank you.

B And what's your name?
Thank you.

Back-up prompts

B Candidate B, what's your surname?
How do you spell it?

Thank you.

A And, Candidate A, what's your surname?
How do you spell it?

Thank you.

How do you write your family / second name?

How do you write your family / second name?

(Ask the following questions. Use candidates' names throughout. Ask Candidate A first.)

Where do you live / come from?

Adult students
Do you work or are you a student in . . .?
What do you do / study?

School-age students
Do you study English at school?
Do you like it?

Thank you.

(Repeat for Candidate B.)

Do you live in . . .?

Have you got a job?
What job do you do? / What subject(s) do you study?

Do you have English lessons?

Test 3

Phase 2
Examiner

(Select one or more questions from the list to ask each candidate. Ask Candidate B first.)

	Back-up prompts
Do you enjoy studying English? Why (not)?	Do you like studying English?
Do you think that English will be useful for you in the future?	Will you use English in the future?
What did you do yesterday evening / last weekend?	Did you do anything yesterday evening / last weekend? What?
What do you enjoy doing in your free time?	What do you like to do in your free time?

Thank you.

(Introduction to Part 2)

In the next part, you are going to talk to each other.

Part 2 (2–3 minutes)

DENTIST'S WAITING ROOM

Tasks Discussing alternatives; expressing opinions; making choices.

Examiner *Say to both candidates:*

> I'm going to describe a situation to you.
>
> A dentist has a room where people wait. It's not very comfortable.
> Talk together about different ways to make the room more comfortable and say which would be best.
>
> Here is a picture with some ideas to help you.

Ask both candidates to look at picture 3A on page V of the Student's Book and repeat the frame.

> I'll say that again.
>
> A dentist has a room where people wait. It's not very comfortable.
> Talk together about different ways to make the room more comfortable and say which would be best.
>
> All right? Talk together.

Allow the candidates enough time to complete the task without intervention. Prompt only if necessary.

Frames for the Speaking test

Part 3 (3 minutes)

VISITING A TOWN

Tasks — Describing people and places; saying where people and things are and what different people are doing.

Examiner — *Say to both candidates:*

> Now, I'd like each of you to talk on your own about something. I'm going to give each of you a photograph of people visiting towns.
>
> Candidate A, here is your photograph. *(Ask Candidate A to look at photo 3B on page VI of the Student's Book.)* Please show it to Candidate B, but I'd like you to talk about it. Candidate B, you just listen. I'll give you your photograph in a moment.
>
> Candidate A, please tell us what you can see in the photograph.

(Candidate A) *Approximately one minute*

If there is a need to intervene, prompts rather than direct questions should be used.

Ask Candidate A to close his/her book.

Examiner

> Now, Candidate B, here is your photograph. It also shows people visiting a town. *(Ask Candidate B to look at photo 3C on page VIII of the Student's Book.)* Please show it to Candidate A and tell us what you can see in the photograph.

(Candidate B) *Approximately one minute*

Ask the candidates to close their books before moving to Part 4.

Part 4 (3 minutes)

Tasks — Talking about one's likes and dislikes; expressing opinions.

Examiner — *Say to both candidates:*

> Your photographs showed people visiting towns. Now, I'd like you to talk together about the things you like to do when you visit a town and say why you like to do them.

Allow the candidates enough time to complete the task without intervention. Prompt only if necessary.

Back-up prompts
1. Talk about the things you like to **do** in a town.
2. Talk about **why** you like to do these things.
3. Talk about **who** you like to visit a town with.
4. Talk about a town you visited **recently**.

> Thank you. That's the end of the test.

TEST 4

Part 1 (2–3 minutes)

Tasks   Identifying oneself; giving information about oneself; talking about interests.

Phase 1
Examiner

A/B   Good morning / afternoon / evening.
Can I have your mark sheets, please?

A/B   I'm ………… and this is ………… .
He / she is just going to listen to us.

A   Now, what's your name?
Thank you.

B   And what's your name?
Thank you.

Back-up prompts

B
Candidate B, what's your surname? How do you spell it? Thank you.

How do you write your family / second name?

A
And, Candidate A, what's your surname? How do you spell it? Thank you.

How do you write your family / second name?

(Ask the following questions. Use candidates' names throughout. Ask Candidate A first.)   Where do you live / come from?   *Adult students*   Do you work or are you a student in . . .?   What do you do / study?   *School-age students*   Do you study English at school?   Do you like it?   Thank you.   *(Repeat for Candidate B.)*

Do you live in . . .?

Have you got a job?
What job do you do? / What subject(s) do you study?

Do you have English lessons?

103

Frames for the Speaking test

Phase 2
Examiner

(Select one or more questions from the list to ask each candidate. Ask Candidate B first.)

	Back-up prompts
Do you enjoy studying English? Why (not)?	Do you like studying English?
Do you think that English will be useful for you in the future?	Will you use English in the future?
What did you do yesterday evening / last weekend?	Did you do anything yesterday evening / last weekend? What?
What do you enjoy doing in your free time?	What do you like to do in your free time?

Thank you.

(Introduction to Part 2)

In the next part, you are going to talk to each other.

Part 2 (2–3 minutes)

AIRPORT PLANNING (SUITABLE FOR GROUPS OF THREE AND PAIRS)

Tasks   Discussing alternatives; expressing opinions; making choices.

Examiner   *Say to both/all candidates:*

> I'm going to describe a situation to you.
>
> A small airport in a tourist area is opening a new building for people to use. Talk together about the things they could put in the building and decide which would be most useful for tourists.
>
> Here is a picture with some ideas to help you.

Ask both/all candidates to look at picture 4A on page VII of the Student's Book and repeat the frame.

> I'll say that again.
>
> A small airport in a tourist area is opening a new building for people to use. Talk together about the things they could put in the building and decide which would be most useful for tourists.
>
> All right? Talk together.

Allow the candidates enough time to complete the task without intervention. Prompt only if necessary.

Test 4

Part 3 (3–4 minutes)

PLAYING A GAME (SUITABLE FOR GROUPS OF THREE AND PAIRS)

Tasks   Describing people and places; saying where people and things are and what different people are doing.

Examiner   *Say to both/all candidates:*

> Now, I'd like each of you to talk on your own about something. I'm going to give each of you a photograph of people playing games.
>
> Candidate A, here is your photograph. (*Ask Candidate A to look at photo 4B on page IV of the Student's Book.*) Please show it to Candidate(s) B (and C), but I'd like you to talk about it. Candidate(s) B (and C), you just listen. I'll give you your photograph(s) in a moment.
>
> Candidate A, please tell us what you can see in the photograph.

(Candidate A)   *Approximately one minute*

If there is a need to intervene, prompts rather than direct questions should be used.

Ask Candidate A to close his/her book.

Examiner

> Now, Candidate B, here is your photograph. It also shows people playing a game. (*Ask Candidate B to look at photo 4C on page VI of the Student's Book.*) Please show it to Candidate(s) A (and C) and tell us what you can see in the photograph.

(Candidate B)   *Approximately one minute*

Ask Candidate B to close his/her book.

Examiner

> Now, Candidate C, here is your photograph. It also shows people playing a game. (*Ask Candidate C to look at photo 4D on page VIII of the Student's Book.*) Please show it to Candidates A and B and tell us what you can see in the photograph.

(Candidate C)   *Approximately one minute*

Ask the candidates to close their books before moving to Part 4.

Part 4 (3–4 minutes)

Tasks   Talking about one's likes and dislikes; expressing opinions.

Examiner   *Say to both/all candidates:*

> Your photographs showed people playing games. Now, I'd like you to talk together about the games you like to play in the house and the games you prefer to play outside.

Allow the candidates enough time to complete the task without intervention. Prompt only if necessary.

Back-up prompts
1. Talk about the games you like to play in the **house**.
2. Talk about the games you prefer to play **outside**.
3. Talk about a game you'd like to **learn**.
4. Talk about when you play **for fun** and when you play **to win**.

> Thank you. That's the end of the test.

Key

Test 1

PAPER 1 READING AND WRITING

READING

Part 1
1 B   2 A   3 C   4 A   5 C

Part 2
6 D   7 E   8 G   9 B   10 C

Part 3
11 B   12 B   13 A   14 A   15 B   16 A   17 A   18 B   19 B   20 A

Part 4
21 C   22 A   23 C   24 B   25 D

Part 5
26 C   27 B   28 D   29 A   30 B   31 C   32 D   33 B   34 C   35 C

WRITING

Part 1
1 mine
2 was
3 pay / spend (just/only)
4 (also) includes
5 (even) larger/bigger than

Part 2

Task-specific Mark Scheme

The content elements that need to be covered are:

i   **information about the object** candidate has just bought
ii reference as to **why** it was purchased
iii mention of **where** candidate will keep / put object **in the bedroom.**

The following sample answers can be used as a guide when marking.

Test 1

SAMPLE A (Test 1, Question 6: Email to a friend)

> Hi Teresa,
>
> I've recently bought a lamp.
>
> It's very nice and it's perfect for my bedroom because it's pink.
>
> I needed it because I love read before sleeping so I'll put it on the nighttable near the bed.
>
> Your Leonie

Examiner Comments

All three parts of the message are clearly communicated.

Mark: 5

SAMPLE B (Test 1, Question 6: Email to a friend)

> Dear Teresa,
> how are you? I told you, that I need a new window for my bedroom... on Monday I went to town and bought a new one! The old window was damaged last winter while the big storm! I couldn't close it anyway! But there was a big problem, it was bigger than the last, so we put it over our bed and not next to the door!
>
> See you in two weeks
>
> xxx Demetrios

Examiner Comments

Although points 1 and 2 are clearly communicated, point 3 requires interpretation by the reader. On the whole the message is communicated.

Mark: 4

Key

SAMPLE C (Test 1, Question 6: Email to a friend)

> Dear Teresa,
>
> I bought a new library for my room. I have need to buy it because this year I have a lot of school's books. I think I put it near my bed. Do you think is a good idea?
>
> Yours Isabella

Examiner Comments

All three parts of the message are attempted. The key word error 'library' requires interpretation by the reader.

Mark: 3

SAMPLE D (Test 1, Question 7: Letter to a friend)

> Dear Alison,
>
> I understand your situation and I have thought of some solutions to help you. Your problem is quite common and I believe every person working in the world has this problem as well. I suggest you do some simple exercise while you are working. You can stretch your arms and legs in order to relax your muscles. You can also control your diets. Try to eat more healthy food for lunch and dinner. Avoid those food that are rich in fats and oils because you are not doing much exercise. I know you may feel tired after work and you may just want to go home and sleep, but I suggest you join a yoga class at least three times a week. Doing yoga can help to relax every parts of your body, including your mind. You can also lose weight because yoga takes up a lot of energy from you. Your feelings can also be expressed under this comfortable condition. Doing yoga really benefits you.
> I hope you can find these suggestions useful. Think positive, don't give too much pressure to yourself!
>
> love Julie

Subscale	Mark	Examiner Comments
Content	5	All content is relevant to the task with appropriate examples and expansion. The target reader is fully informed.
Communicative Achievement	5	The conventions of the communicative task (consistently appropriate register and letter format are used) to hold the target reader's attention and communicate straightforward ideas clearly and effectively.
Organisation	4	Although sentences tend to be short and paragraphing is minimal, the text is connected and coherent, using a variety of linking words (*and; also; as well; because*) and some cohesive devices (this *problem*; *in order to*; these *suggestions*).
Language	5	A range of everyday and some less common lexis is used appropriately (*your problem is quite common; relax your muscles; lose weight*). These are some minor errors, particularly with collocation (*yoga takes up a lot of energy from you; don't give too much pressure to yourself*) which occur when attempting less common lexis.
		A range of simple and some complex grammatical forms (*I suggest you do some simple exercise while you are working; Avoid those food that are rich in fats; Doing yoga can help to relax...; Your feelings can also be expressed*) are used with a good degree of control. Errors are minimal and do not impede communication (*control your diets; avoid those food; every parts of your body*).

Key

SAMPLE E (Test 1, Question 7: Letter to a friend)

> Dear Alice,
>
> I am really happy about your new job. I can understand you well about it because I know you love a sport and your figure. Anyway that is not end of the world. Firstable, try on your lunch break going out and move a little bit – for example doing shooping. Secendly, after work you can always go to the gym and do some exercises or buy a Wii. There are a lot of exercises which you can do at home for free and really enjoy it. Believe me I am doing this and really is help me.
>
> I hope I could help you a little bit and you will choose something.
>
> Amelia, xx

Scales	Mark	Commentary
Content	5	All content is relevant to the task, with appropriate examples and good expansion. The target reader is fully informed.
Communicative Achievement	5	The conventions of the communicative task are used to hold the target reader's attention (suitable letter format and consistently appropriate register). Straightforward ideas are communicated clearly and effectively.
Organisation	4	Despite limited paragraphing, the text is connected and coherent. A variety of linking words (*because; Secondly; for example; and; or*) and cohesive devices (*I can understand you well about it; anyway; There are a lot of exercises* which *you can do at home; I am doing* this) are used with reasonable success, although there are some errors (*Firstable; a lot of exercises . . . enjoy it*).
Language	3	In general, everyday vocabulary is used appropriately, despite some errors of spelling (*shooping; Secendly*). There is some attempt at using less common lexis (*your figure; that is not end of the world; do some exercises*). Simple grammatical forms are used with a good degree of control (*I am really happy about your new job; after work you can always go to the gym; I hope ... you will choose something*). Errors are noticeable (*love a sport; try on your lunch break going out; I am doing this and really is help me; I hope I could help you a little bit*) but they do not impede communication.

SAMPLE F (Test 1, Question 7: Letter to a friend)

> Hi there,
>
> I receive your letter. I think you should go walkin to the job and you should have hilthey food you should stop eat fast food and frayd food you should go to the jem tow days week or go out with your friends and play any sport football or swimming. you should stop eatting candy. When you wake up you should do some exercise or in the weekend you can go walking or do any another spor and you sould start som dait. If you do what. . .

Scales	Mark	Commentary
Content	5	The candidate has addressed the task fully, giving all the information required. The target reader is fully informed.
Communicative Achievement	3	Although the reader may struggle to follow the message in the second sentence, register and format are generally appropriate, and straightforward ideas are communicated using the conventions of the task.
Organisation	2	The text is connected using basic, high-frequency linking words (*and*; *or*) and a limited number of cohesive devices (*When you wake up*; *any* another *spor*). The text is largely coherent, but limited punctuation causes some difficulty for the target reader, especially in the long second sentence.
Language	3	In general, everyday vocabulary is used appropriately. Errors are mainly with spelling but the meaning can still be determined (*hilthey*; *frayd food*; *go to the jem tow days week*; *start som dait*). A limited range of simple grammatical forms (largely restricted to *you should*) is used with good control (*I think ... you should go to the jem*; *When you wake up you should do some exercise*). Errors are noticeable, but the meaning is still clear (*I receive your letter*; *you should stop eat*).

111

Key

SAMPLE G (Test 1, Question 8: Story)

> DISCOVERED MEMORIES
>
> When I sat down, I discovered I was next to someone very famous. "You know this face!" I thought. Yes! It was Brian May the best guitar player of the rockgroup "Queen". Well, he still plays amazing good even he is 62 years old. WOW! I looked up again and now I saw his best friend Roger Taylor — the drumer. He is one of the best drumer in the world — which is a fact.
> "What shall I do now?"
> Brian looked at me now.
> "Aren't you the girl, who smiled at me in Hamburg at the concert 2008?"
>
> Amazing. . . he remembered me. . . !

Scales	Mark	Commentary
Content	5	The story continues naturally from the prompt sentence. Despite the lack of a clear ending, the target reader can follow the storyline easily.
Communicative Achievement	5	The conventions of storytelling are used in an appropriate register to hold the target reader's attention throughout. There is an effective use of direct speech when expressing the writer's thoughts and recalling the conversation with Brian May.
Organisation	5	The text is generally well-organised using a limited number of linking words (and *now I saw*) together with a variety of more sophisticated cohesive devices (pronouns, *You know* this *face!*; It *was Brian May*; which *is a fact*). Although there are some errors with linking (*even he is 62; the girl, who smiled*), the text is coherent throughout.
Language	4	Despite some minor spelling errors (*drumer*) a range of everyday lexis is used appropriately. A range of simple grammatical forms (past and present tenses, question forms) is used with a good degree of control. Errors are minimal and they do not impede communication (*he still plays amazing good*).

SAMPLE H (Test 1, Question 8: Story)

> WHEN I SAT DOWN, I DISCOVERED THAT I WAS NEXT TO SOMEONE VERY FAMOUS, AT THE BIGINING I DIDN'T REALIZED WHO IT WAS. EVERYONE CAME AROUND HIM AND START TAKING LOT OF PICTURE OF HIM THEN I ASK THIS YOUNG MAN AND HE TOLD THAT IT WAS A SINGER, CALLED ENRIQUE IGLESIAS THEN I THOUGHT HOW STUPID I WAS BECAUSE I DIDN'T RECOGNIZED HIM AND HE WAS THE BEST SINGER EVER IN THE WORLD ALL THE GIRL WILL BE JEALOUS OF ME BECAUSE THEY LOVE HIM. THEN I STARTED TALKING WITH HIM AND HE WAS REALLY NICE SO WE HAD LUNCH TOGETHER AND IT WAS SO FUN. THEN I WOKE UP.

Scales	Mark	Commentary
Content	5	The story continues logically from the prompt sentence. The target reader would be able to follow the story.
Communicative Achievement	4	The story format is appropriate and a suitable register is used consistently. Problems with punctuation mean the target reader has to read the text closely to follow the storyline at times, for example, the long sentence beginning *Everyone came around him ... because they love him.*
Organisation	4	A variety of linking words (*at the bigining; then; because; and; so we had lunch together*) and cohesive devices (*who it was; everyone came around him; a singer, called Enrique Iglesias*) are used. Some errors of punctuation and a lack of paragraphing affect the overall organisation and confuse the reader at times (for example, in the second long sentence).
Language	4	A range of everyday and some less common lexis is used appropriately (*realized; taking . . . picture; recognized; jealous*). In general, a range of simple and some more complex grammatical forms (relative clauses; use of gerunds; superlative forms) are used with reasonable control. A number of errors are present but they do not impede communication (*I didn't realized; start taking lot of picture; it was so fun*).

Key

SAMPLE I (Test 1, Question 8: Story)

> When I sat down, I discovered I was next to someone very famous. It happend when was at Luton airport I wanted for my mum she came from Brazil. When had one our to wait she arrive. I was soo tired when I soy somethin different everebody came to me and take picture of me when I looked arroud didn't belived. It's Michael Jackson his was there, vav!!! A lot of securit fans. He sat besaid me, but I didn't taked picture from he becouse I forgot my camera, and his gone.
>
> My mum arrive, but never will forgot tha day.

Scales	Mark	Commentary
Content	5	The story continues logically from the prompt sentence. The target reader would be able to follow the story.
Communicative Achievement	3	Although the target reader has to work hard at times to follow the storyline, for example in the second and fourth sentences, an appropriate story format and register is used to communicate straightforward ideas.
Organisation	3	The text is connected and is largely coherent using basic linking words *(when; but; because)* and a limited number of cohesive devices (It *happend* when *was*; He *sat besaid me*). However, lack of punctuation causes problems for the target reader at times, particularly in the fourth sentence.
Language	2	In general, everyday vocabulary is used appropriately. Errors are largely with spelling: in some cases meaning can still be determined *(one our; everebody; arroud; securit; besaid)*, however, there are other cases where the meaning is obscured *(I wanted for my mum; I soy somethin)*. Simple grammatical forms are used with reasonable control, although there are repeated problems with past tenses. A number of errors are present which distract the reader at times *(When had one our to wait she arrive; It's Michael Jackson his was there)*.

PAPER 2   LISTENING

Part 1

1 C   2 C   3 B   4 B   5 A   6 C   7 B

Part 2

8 C   9 B   10 A   11 A   12 C   13 C

Part 3

14 Greenland
15 Five/5 o'clock (p.m./in the afternoon)
   5 pm
   17.00 (hours)
   5.00pm
16 computer(s)
17 space(-)ship
18 top/highest
19 F/fri(day)

Part 4

20 B   21 A   22 A   23 B   24 B   25 B

Key

Test 1 transcript

This is the Cambridge Preliminary English Test, Test 1. There are four parts to the test. You will hear each part twice. For each part of the test there will be time for you to look through the questions and time for you to check your answers.

Write your answers on the question paper. You will have six minutes at the end of the test to copy your answers onto the answer sheet.

The recording will now be stopped. Please ask any questions now, because you must not speak during the test.

[Pause]

Now open your question paper and look at Part 1.

PART 1   *There are seven questions in this part. For each question there are three pictures and a short recording. Choose the correct picture and put a tick in the box below it.*

Before we start, here is an example.

Where is the girl's hat?

Mum: Where's your new hat, Sally? I hope you haven't left it on the school bus.

Sally: Don't worry, Mum. I put it in my school bag because I was too hot.

Mum: Are you sure? I can't see it there. You probably dropped it in the road somewhere.

Sally: Oh, here it is – hanging in the hall. I forgot to take it this morning.

[Pause]

The first picture is correct so there is a tick in box A.

Look at the three pictures for question 1 now.

[Pause]

Now we are ready to start. Listen carefully. You will hear each recording twice.

One. How will they book their flights?

Man: So what about our flights then, shall I book on the internet? Or do you want to go to a travel agent's?

Woman: Well, actually, I've already been to the travel agent's and got some prices . . . They can offer us a better price than anything I've seen on the internet.

Man: Great . . . well let's make a decision and then go ahead and book. We could phone them, couldn't we? Or is it better to pop in?

Woman: I'd prefer not to phone because I want to pay in cash.

Man: Okay.

[Pause]

Now listen again.

[The recording is repeated]

[Pause]

Two. What has the daughter forgotten to bring on holiday?

Girl: Mmm . . . nice bathroom in this hotel! Can I borrow your shampoo, Mum? I left mine at home.

Mum: Okay, but put it back in my bag when you've finished.

Girl: And I don't believe it! I must have forgotten to bring my hairbrush, too. I can't find it anywhere in my suitcase. I was sure I'd put it in!

Mum: You had! I've already put it in the bathroom with your other washing things. I don't

Test 1

know why you brought toothpaste though. We certainly didn't need two tubes! We're only here for four days.

[Pause]

Now listen again.

[The recording is repeated]

[Pause]

Three. What will the man and woman do on Sunday?

Woman: Oh, I'm so tired! Shall we just stay at home this weekend? Maybe watch some DVDs and read the newspapers?

Man: Mmm . . . how about going to the beach tomorrow with a picnic as it's so hot . . . although we really ought to clean the flat. Oh, I nearly forgot! Isn't your sister coming to see us on Sunday?

Woman: Yes, you're right . . . she is! She'll enjoy a good day at the seaside, won't she? We'll relax at home another time . . . and then do the housework, too!

Man: Sounds great!

[Pause]

Now listen again.

[The recording is repeated]

[Pause]

Four. Which blouse does the girl decide to buy?

Girl: Tom, I need your opinion about this blouse. I like the collar, but the sleeves are rather long.

Tom: Um . . . I'm not sure. Look at some more before you decide. What about this one? Short sleeves, no collar.

Girl: It's a bit ordinary. I do agree, though, it's elegant. Ah, here's one with a collar and without sleeves, but it isn't quite so nice as the other one. Hmm . . . no, I like the first one I saw. I can always make the sleeves shorter.

Tom: Okay. I think it's a good choice.

[Pause]

Now listen again.

[The recording is repeated]

[Pause]

Five. When is the girl having a party?

Amanda: Hello, this is Amanda. About my birthday party. I told you it was on the fifteenth, but I've got to change it to the thirteenth. That's a Thursday, which I know isn't perfect. But no-one can come on Friday the fourteenth because it's the school disco. Sorry about the change, but Mum and Dad have got something planned for me on the fifteenth. Anyway, the party's at my house, and it's starting about eight o'clock. Call me back and let me know if you can come.

[Pause]

Now listen again.

[The recording is repeated]

[Pause]

Six. Where is the motorcycle race going to finish?

Man: This year's motorcycle race will finish in the city centre. Hundreds of people are expected to be in the square in front of the town hall to watch the finish of the race

117

Key

on Saturday afternoon. For those who'd like to see the bikes in action, seating will be provided in the square outside the stadium. Race organisers recommend that from Castle Square, with its position on top of the hill, there'll be a good view of the bikes making their way through the city.

[Pause]

Now listen again.

[The recording is repeated]

[Pause]

Seven. What will the woman repair next?

Boy: I really want to go out on my bike, but it's got a flat tyre. Can you fix it?

Woman: I'm really busy at the moment. Oh, and we don't have anything to repair it with. Can't you do something else? Why don't you play football instead?

Boy: But the football's flat as well.

Woman: Oh. But it just needs more air. That shouldn't take too long. I've just finished putting some new glass in the window so I'll have a coffee and then I'll do it.

[Pause]

Now listen again.

[The recording is repeated]

[Pause]

That is the end of Part 1.

[Pause]

PART 2   *Now turn to Part 2, questions 8 to 13.*

You will hear a radio interview with a man called Robin Marshall, who has written a book about Argentina.

For each question, put a tick in the correct box.

You now have 45 seconds to look at the questions for Part 2.

[Pause]

Now we are ready to start. Listen carefully. You will hear the recording twice.

Int: Today I'm with Robin Marshall, who has just written a book about travelling in Argentina. Robin, tell us about yourself . . .

Robin: Well, I've travelled to South America a lot for my work and I know Argentina well now. So well that I could be a tour guide if I wanted! I speak fluent Spanish, so I don't need anyone to translate for me. My job involves travelling around selling products for my company. I meet a lot of people doing that, and I wanted to share those experiences with others, so I decided to try writing.

Int: So, tell us about your last visit to Argentina. What was the weather like?

Robin: Well, it was winter there, so mornings were cold, but I'd expected that. Every day they said on the radio that it would be sunny later and sure enough, it was! I wanted to go sightseeing, and the weather was perfect for that.

Int: And where did you go when you went sightseeing?

Robin: Well, I went to a wonderful market that sold everything from modern art to old records of traditional music, which I collect. I came home with a beautiful painting of the area. I also saw a wonderful antique chair, but unfortunately it was too big to bring back.

Int: Now, Argentina is famous for its dancing. Did you see any performances during your trip?

Robin: I did, yes. It reminded me of when I used to attend dance classes. I enjoyed them although I was never very good. I'm sure my teacher was pleased when I said

		I wasn't going to continue! But these dancers made it look so easy that at that moment I felt like joining in and dancing with them.
	Int:	It sounds wonderful! And what else did you do?
	Robin:	Well, I went to a small village on the coast. I took the bus there, and got a room in a small hotel. The hotel owner was very friendly. He took me down the river in his boat. It was very beautiful – you could see the forest in the distance.
	Int:	Do you have a favourite place in Argentina?
	Robin:	Definitely. It's a mountain near Buenos Aires. It's famous for its spectacular scenery. But when I went there it was very misty and the sun was just rising. You couldn't see much: there were no birds or animals about. It was totally quiet, and I loved that. I shall go back one day.
	Int:	We look forward to reading your book. Thank you, Robin.
	Robin:	Thank you.

[Pause]

Now listen again.

[The recording is repeated]

[Pause]

That is the end of Part 2.

[Pause]

PART 3   *Now turn to Part 3, questions 14 to 19.*

You will hear a radio presenter talking about a museum where you can see a new film.

For each question, fill in the missing information in the numbered space.

You now have 20 seconds to look at Part 3.

[Pause]

Now we are ready to start. Listen carefully. You will hear the recording twice.

Int:	Next on the programme, we're offering free tickets to go and see a brand new film called *A Year in Greenland*. The film, which tells you all about the plants and animals in that wonderful country, has won a prize at the national film festival – it's well worth seeing.
	The film can only be seen at a fantastic new cinema that has just been completed inside the Science Museum in the city centre. It's showing this Sunday with performances every hour from midday onwards, with the last showing at five o'clock, two hours before the museum closes at seven. So there's six times to choose from.
	So why not take the whole family to the museum this Sunday – there's lots to do. Children will want to head straight down to the basement where the computers are kept. I promise you they'll come away with all sorts of exciting pictures they've created.
	Moving to the first floor, a working steam engine and a life-sized model of a space-ship are among the favourite exhibits, and these are popular with people of all ages, not just children.
	And if you get thirsty or if you want to have lunch out, there's an excellent café with wonderful views of the city on the top floor of the building.
	Entrance to the museum is free on Sundays, but it would normally cost £3.25 to go and see the film. To get your free tickets, you should email this programme by midday on Friday. We've only got a limited number of tickets, so the earlier you contact us, the more likely you are to get one. We'll then get back in email contact with you before 12 o'clock on Saturday if you've been successful.
	So have a pencil and paper ready after this song.

[Pause]

Now listen again.

Key

[The recording is repeated]

[Pause]

That is the end of Part 3.

[Pause]

PART 4 *Now turn to Part 4, questions 20 to 25.*

Look at the six sentences for this part. You will hear two neighbours, a woman, Natasha, and a man, Colin, talking about running.

Decide if each sentence is correct or incorrect. If it is correct, put a tick in the box under A for YES. If it is not correct, put a tick in the box under B for NO.

You now have 20 seconds to look at the questions for Part 4.

[Pause]

Now we are ready to start. Listen carefully. You will hear the recording twice.

Colin: Hi Natasha. I see you're going out for a run. You're lucky you don't have to go to work today.

Natasha: Hello Colin – I *am* going to the office, but I've started running to work instead of taking the bus. It means I can keep fit and save some money.

Colin: I tried running to work for a while, but I didn't like breathing in all the traffic pollution and I kept getting coughs. I soon went back to using public transport. I keep fit at the gym.

Natasha: Well, I've found a route that avoids most of the main roads.

Colin: But it's still almost five kilometres – and it must be dangerous.

Natasha: That's why I choose quiet streets. If I could, I'd run in the country – that would be lovely, but it would mean leaving it till the weekends. Running gives me a wonderful feeling of freedom – it's just what I need before sitting down in the office every day.

Colin: But surely you don't wear your tracksuit and trainers at work?

Natasha: Oh – I keep a suit at the office and change when I arrive. I think it's important to look professional so I don't mind at all.

Colin: Anyway, since you're so fit, are you going to join in the big race next month?

Natasha: I'd like to. What's the distance?

Colin: Twenty kilometres – anyone can enter and there are prizes for different age groups.

Natasha: Even if I come last, it will still be good fun – running on your own can sometimes get quite lonely. Are you going to take part?

Colin: Oh yes, I've sent in my application form already – I'll get one for you. But I'm not going to train by running to work – I'll run round the park a few times when I get home in the evenings – that's safer!

Natasha: Okay. Anyway I must go now or I'll be late. Bye.

[Pause]

Now listen again.

[The recording is repeated]

[Pause]

That is the end of Part 4.

[Pause]

You now have six minutes to check and copy your answers on to the answer sheet.

Note: Teacher, stop the recording here and time six minutes. Remind students when there is **one** minute remaining.

That is the end of the test.

120

Test 2

PAPER 1   READING AND WRITING

READING

Part 1
1 A   2 C   3 B   4 C   5 A

Part 2
6 C   7 H   8 A   9 F   10 D

Part 3
11 B   12 A   13 A   14 B   15 B   16 A   17 B   18 A   19 A   20 B

Part 4
21 C   22 B   23 A   24 B   25 D

Part 5
26 C   27 A   28 C   29 A   30 B   31 B   32 D   33 A   34 D   35 C

WRITING

Part 1

1 to fill
2 did you do/have you done/did you have/have you had
3 not to be/arrive/come
   to avoid being/arriving/coming
4 (much/really/would) prefer
5 give

Part 2

Task-specific Mark Scheme

The content elements that need to be covered are:

i   **reason** for absence from school next week
ii **apology** for absence
iii **request** for information about next week's **work.**

The following sample answers can be used as a guide when marking.

Key

SAMPLE A (Test 2, Question 6: Note to your teacher)

> Dear, Mrs David,
> I think I will be absent from English class next week because next week is my best friend's birthday so I have to go his party. I'm really sorry it won't happen again. Can you tell me about next week's work?
> I have to be ready.
> Qiang Shu

Examiner Comments

All three parts of the message are clearly communicated.

Mark: 5

SAMPLE B (Test 2, Question 6: Note to your teacher)

> Good morning teacher,
>
> I want say to her, that next week I will be absent in her class, because I will do a Spanish Exam, The "Cervntes", it will be in the morning, so I will be absent. I'm so apologise, because her lessons are very interesting. I would ask her, what will she do next class, and if she can, sending me the material.
>
> Thank you
>
> Gisella

Examiner Comments

Although all points have been attempted, errors in pronoun use impede understanding.

Mark: 3

SAMPLE C (Test 2, Question 6: Note to your teacher)

> Dear Teacher,
>
> I am going to be absent becuse I made very much nois in the lesson. I am very sorry, I made noises in the class. I hope you are not upset with me. Can you please send me some information about the homework.
>
> Elin

Examiner Comments

Although all three parts of the message have been attempted, the context is unclear.

Mark: 2

Key

SAMPLE D (Test 2, Question 7: Letter to a friend)

> Dear Jenna,
>
> How are you? Long time no see! I have many friends. As my mother always says, friends are important in our life. As I spend most of my time at work, I have plenty of friends there. Being friends, we can help each other. if we get some difficultie at work. If I have a personal problem, friends are important in that moment. They can advice me about life. So, we can't live without friends.
>
> I'm happy to be your friend also So, I'm looking forward to hearing more about your friend.
>
> Best wishes
>
> Makena

Scales	Mark	Commentary
Content	5	All content is relevant to the task. The target reader is fully informed.
Communicative Achievement	5	Register and format are consistently appropriate to the task. Ideas are communicated effectively and the letter holds the reader's attention throughout.
Organisation	4	Although sentences tend to be short the text is generally well-organised and coherent and there is appropriate use of paragraphing. A limited number of linking words (*also*; *So*) and a variety of cohesive devices (As *my mother always says; I have plenty of friends* there; *friends are important in* that *moment;* They *can advice me*) are used. Some errors of punctuation distract in places (*we can help each other. if we get some difficultie; I'm happy to be your friend also So, I'm looking forward to hearing more . . .*).
Language	4	A range of both everyday and less common lexis is used appropriately (*Long time no see; I spend most of my time at work; plenty of friends; we can't live without friends*). Simple grammatical forms are used with a good degree of control (though these are mainly limited to the present tense), and there is some evidence of more complex grammatical forms (*If I have a personal problem . . .; I'm looking forward to hearing more . . .*). Errors are minimal and non-impeding errors (*difficultie; They can advice me*).

SAMPLE E (Test 2, Question 7: Letter to a friend)

Dear Jenna,

Thanks for your letter, that made me really happy! At first, I want to know more about your friend, tell me more in your next letter! I've got a lot of friends. But I've got (maybe) 10 close friends who I spend a lot of time with. Most weekends we all together and spend our time with watching TV, talking, going in pubs or clubs and so on. I am really happy to have them. They are all the most important for me (after my family). But at the moment I'm in London (you know) so I can't see them. But I fligh home in 12 day and then I see them 2 weeks. You don't believe how happy I am about this! Ok Jenna, I need to go back to work.

I hope I hear you soon.

Best wishes

Marianna

Scales	Mark	Commentary
Content	5	All content points are addressed with appropriate expansion. The target reader is fully informed.
Communicative Achievement	5	Uses the conventions of the letter and consistent register and format to communicate straightforward ideas. There is good use of a natural, informal tone holds the reader's attention.
Organisation	4	A variety of cohesive devices (*Thanks for your letter,* that *made me really happy;* 10 close friends *who I;* They *are all;* how happy I am about *this*) and a limited range of linking words (*At first; But; and; so*) are used. The text is connected and coherent, but the lack of paragraphing affects the overall organisation.
Language	4	A range of everyday and some less common lexis (*made me really happy; close friends*) is used. There are some errors of usage (*At first; going in pubs; I fligh home*) but the meaning is not obscured. A range of simple grammatical forms (present and past tenses) and some more complex grammatical forms (present perfect; imperative forms; relative clauses) are used with a good degree of control. Errors are noticeable but meaning can still be determined (*Most weekends we all together; spend our time with watching; I see them 2 weeks; You don't believe how happy I am*).

Key

SAMPLE F (Test 2, Question 7: Letter to a friend)

> Hi Jenna, how are you? long time, I didn't see yoo. How was your holiday this year. I went in Mallorca for a swimming cours. it was fantastic but I missed my friends. I meet there a lot of new people but I was there alone and with other people we don't have a lot of common things. I want to have fun but other mate were so quiet. They read the book or listenig music when we had a free time. So now I feel good because I have my friends next to me. We have lot of fun and also common things it was good experience for my life I hope see you soon. take care.
>
> Christopher

Scales	Mark	Commentary
Content	3	There is some irrelevance as the writer has written about friends on one particular occasion rather than in general, but the task is addressed and the target reader is, on the whole, informed.
Communicative Achievement	4	Uses the conventions of the communicative task (appropriate register, attempt at letter format) to communicate straightforward ideas.
Organisation	3	The text is connected and coherent but word order and punctuation are not always appropriate (for example in the sentence beginning *I meet there a lot of new people* and the final long sentence) and the lack of paragraphing means the reader has to work at following the message at times.
		Basic linking words (*but; and; when; so; because*) and a limited number of cohesive devices are used (*it was fantastic; I meet there a lot of new people; They read the book*).
Language	3	In general, everyday vocabulary is used appropriately. There are several spelling errors (*yoo; cours; listenig*), but these do not impede communication. There is some attempt at using less common lexis (*we don't have a lot of common things*).
		Simple grammatical forms are used with reasonable control. Errors are noticeable, especially with tenses, but the meaning can still be determined (*long time, I didn't see yoo; I want to have fun; They read the book or listenig music*).

SAMPLE G (Test 2, Question 8: Story)

> It was getting dark and I was completely lost. I knew that I was in the wood, but I could not find my way. I tryed to use my mobile phone but there was no signal. I was about to cry when I heard a very strange and gloomy noise. It was comming from the darkest corner of the wood. At first, I saw nothing but after a second quick look I realized that there was something wich was gazing at me. Despite the fact that I knew it was the time to run away, I was totally unable to move. I was sure it was the end, when I saw the forest officer comming.

Scales	Mark	Commentary
Content	5	The story continues effectively from the prompt. The target reader would be able to follow the story without any problem.
Communicative Achievement	5	There is a clear communication which holds the target reader's attention throughout and a consistently appropriate register and format are used.
Organisation	4	The text is generally well-organised and coherent, although there is limited connection between sentences. Linking words (*and; but; when; At first;*) and cohesive devices (It *was comming from;* there was something *wich* was gazing at me; Despite the fact that) are used, but the range is quite limited.
Language	5	There is a good range of both everyday and less common vocabulary (*completely lost; there was no signal; gloomy noise; gazing*). There are minor spelling errors (*tryed; wich; comming*) but these do not impede communication. A range of simple and some complex grammatical forms (i.e. range of narrative tenses) are used with a good degree of control.

Key

SAMPLE H (Test 2, Question 8: Story)

> It was getting dark and I was completely lost. The street was almos empty. I saw an old man walking on the river bank, but when I was walking towards him, he jumped in the river. I tryed to stop him, but it was too late, I was very confuse I didn't know what I could do, so I jumped in the river too. and I catched him. he said to me, please let me go, I don't want to live any more, but I couldn't do it. I took him out from the river he was crying. I asked him why he wanted to kill himself? He answered me that his wife had died and he doesn't want to live with out her I said to him don't be affray you must continue with your life. He cryed this time more and said; Thanks I think that you have reason, I must to continue with my life.

Scales	Mark	Commentary
Content	5	The story continues naturally from the prompt sentence and is fully developed with a clear ending. The target reader would be able to follow the story with no problem.
Communicative Achievement	5	The storyline is communicated effectively using an appropriate register and format and holding the target reader's attention throughout.
Organisation	4	The story is generally well-organised and coherent, although there are noticeable errors with punctuation, for example in the sixth line from *and I catched him* and the long sentence beginning *He answered me*. A limited range of linking words (*and; but; so*) and cohesive devices are used. These are mainly restricted to pronouns (*walking towards* him, he *jumped; but I couldn't do* it; *live with out* her).
Language	4	Despite a number of spelling errors (*almos; tryed; affray; cryed*), a range of everyday vocabulary is used appropriately. There is some evidence of less common lexis (*It was getting dark and I was completely lost; the river bank; let me go*). A range of simple grammatical and some more complex grammatical forms (for example a range of narrative tenses, modals and indirect question forms) are used. A number of errors are present (*I catched him; he doesn't want to live with out her; I must to continue with my life*) but there is reasonable control and the errors do not impede communication.

SAMPLE I (Test 2, Question 8: Story)

> It was getting dark and I was completely lost. I was so worry about it. Because, that time I had stolen my bag. The weather was terrible. It was chilly and cloudy. So I felt very bad. Suddenly, I tought one of my friend. She lived close to there. So I called her, she could help me. A month late I changed my mind. This city is very exciting and interesting. Now, I forget that time. I'm really enjoying this time. Because I can meet many other country's friend and I can share their experience. So, now I'm so happy.

Scales	Mark	Commentary
Content	5	The story continues from the prompt and the target reader is, on the whole, informed.
Communicative Achievement	3	Ideas are communicated using an appropriate format and register. However, the target reader would have to work to follow the storyline at times (particularly towards the middle when it says *A month later I changed my mind*).
Organisation	3	The story is connected and largely coherent, although it is slightly disjointed at times due to the short sentences.
		Basic linking words (*Because; So; and*) and a limited number of cohesive devices (*It was chilly; Suddenly; She lived close to there; that time; ... this time*) are used.
Language	3	In general, everyday and some less common lexis (*chilly and cloudy; I changed my mind; share their experience*) are used appropriately.
		Simple grammatical forms are used with reasonable control.
		Errors are noticeable but in general, the meaning can still be determined (*I tought one of my friend; I had stolen my bag*).

Key

PAPER 2   LISTENING

Part 1
1 B   2 B   3 C   4 A   5 A   6 C   7 C

Part 2
8 C   9 A   10 B   11 C   12 A   13 B

Part 3
14 artists
15 12th July
16 Fridays
17 groups
18 lessons
19 timetable

Part 4
20 B   21 B   22 A   23 B   24 B   25 A

Test 2

Test 2 transcript

This is the Cambridge Preliminary English Test, Test 2. There are four parts to the test. You will hear each part twice. For each part of the test there will be time for you to look through the questions and time for you to check your answers.

Write your answers on the question paper. You will have six minutes at the end of the test to copy your answers onto the answer sheet.

The recording will now be stopped. Please ask any questions now, because you must not speak during the test.

[Pause]

Now open your question paper and look at Part 1.

PART 1 *There are seven questions in this part. For each question there are three pictures and a short recording. Choose the correct picture and put a tick in the box below it.*

Before we start, here is an example.

How did the woman get to work?

Woman: Oh, I'm so sorry I'm late – I missed the bus. I was trying to decide whether to walk or go back and get my bike when I saw my neighbour. Luckily he offered me a lift, because he works near here.

[Pause]

The first picture is correct so there is a tick in box A.

Look at the three pictures for question 1 now.

[Pause]

Now we are ready to start. Listen carefully. You will hear each recording twice.

One. What has the boy lost?

Boy: Mum – I love it here. The city's really interesting and it's quite easy to find my way round, thanks to the map you gave me – I don't know what I'd do without it. I've taken some great photos, but I left my camera on a tram so I won't be able to show you! And things are more expensive than I expected, so I don't think my money will last very long. Can you send me some more? Thanks. Speak to you again soon.

[Pause]

Now listen again.

[The recording is repeated]

[Pause]

Two. What time does the race begin?

Boy: I'm running the race on Saturday, but I don't know where it is or when it begins.

Man: Well, you're going to run round the lake. All the runners have to meet in the car park and register by quarter to two, though the race won't actually start until half past. There should be about a hundred runners.

Boy: When will it be over? I've got to catch a train at quarter past three.

Man: It's 15 kilometres! You won't be on time for that!

[Pause]

Now listen again.

[The recording is repeated]

[Pause]

131

Key

Three. Which musical instrument does the boy play now?

Girl: Look at this notice. The school's starting trumpet lessons next term.

Boy: Oh, the trumpet! That's an instrument I'd love to play. It's got a great sound.

Girl: Yes, I might try that, or maybe piano, I don't know. You learnt piano, didn't you?

Boy: Yes, I played the piano for years, in fact – until I took up the drums last year. You can't do everything, and I just felt they were more my sort of instrument, really.

[Pause]

Now listen again.

[The recording is repeated]

[Pause]

Four. What will the weather be like tomorrow afternoon?

Woman: And now for tomorrow's weather. The day will start showery and windy. Those winds should disappear by late morning, but the wet weather will continue until well into the evening. Although we might see some bright sunny periods between the showers early on, by midday it will be cloudy, with temperatures of no more than ten or twelve degrees centigrade.

[Pause]

Now listen again.

[The recording is repeated]

[Pause]

Five. What is the subject of James Wilson's book?

Man: This latest book by James Wilson is part of a series of practical guides for young people written by experts. The first in the series, *Cookery for Beginners*, was written by a well-known television cook. It's very clear and well written, and is a best-seller. Wilson's book, *Computers for Beginners* is in the bookshops now and is also very popular. And there'll be a book about photography called *Photography for Beginners*, which will come out next year. It's written by a newspaper cameraman and will certainly be full of useful information.

[Pause]

Now listen again.

[The recording is repeated]

[Pause]

Six. Which part of the man's body hurts him at the moment?

Doctor: It's been four weeks since your accident, hasn't it? So tell me how you are feeling. How's the pain in your legs?

Man: My legs were really hurting me until last week, but that's worn off now, I'm glad to say. So has the pain in my back. My shoulder's still fairly sore, though not as bad as it was, fortunately.

Doctor: I'm pleased to hear that. Let's take a look at you, anyway.

[Pause]

Now listen again.

[The recording is repeated]

[Pause]

Seven. Where was the man's knowledge of Spanish useful?

Woman: How was your trip, Peter?

Man: Great. I was glad I learnt some Spanish before I went.

Test 2

	Woman:	Did you manage to order a meal in a restaurant?
	Man:	Well, I was staying with English friends actually, and I just ate at home with them. I did manage to explain what I wanted when I went shopping though, and I was pleased about that. But I didn't manage to talk to any of the Spanish people who were invited to my friends' place – that was really disappointing. I couldn't understand what they said to me.

[Pause]

Now listen again.

[The recording is repeated]

[Pause]

That is the end of Part 1.

[Pause]

PART 2   *Now turn to Part 2, questions 8 to 13.*

You will hear a radio interview with a man called Harry Park, who is talking about the adventure travel company he runs.

For each question, put a tick in the correct box.

You now have 45 seconds to look at the questions for Part 2.

[Pause]

Now we are ready to start. Listen carefully. You will hear the recording twice.

Int:	Harry Park, you run a travel company which organises adventure holidays in some difficult places. How did you first become interested in 'adventure travel'?
Harry:	Well, my father worked in an insurance company once he had a family. But before that he'd spent several years travelling the world, and he never stopped telling us about it. His stories were much more exciting than the books I read, and they made me want to travel and have adventures of my own.
Int:	And what made you decide to start an adventure travel company?
Harry:	Well, when I was in my twenties, I travelled a lot in different countries. I went exploring and climbing in mountains and deserts. I wanted to show other people how wonderful these things were. The business has been very successful, but when I started it I didn't know if I'd make any money.
Int:	Your company's called *Far and Wide*. How did you choose the name?
Harry:	Well, I just called it *Park Travel* at first. But everyone thought that was terribly boring! My wife kept suggesting different things, but in the end it was a customer who gave me the idea. *Far and Wide* is also the title of a book that a friend wrote, so it reminds me of him, too.
Int:	Great . . . The places you visit are usually very unspoilt, Harry. Some people think it's not a good idea to take tourists there. What would you say to them?
Harry:	Well, most of the places we visit have no inhabitants, so we aren't going to spoil people's way of life, or bring in things like television and fridges! And I make sure that we always take care of the environment. We are careful not to cause pollution, so we take all our rubbish away.
Int:	Some of the things you do are also dangerous. Do you enjoy danger?
Harry:	Well, it's not a question of enjoying it – it's just that you can't do what I do without thinking about the possible dangers. I'm never frightened though. If I'm taking a group up a mountain or something like that, I just concentrate on what I have to do and get on with it.

133

Key

	Int:	You've been to some fascinating places, Harry. What's your favourite?
	Harry:	It's in India. You travel along a river through spectacular scenery and up into the mountains in Madhya Pradesh. In the valley on the other side there's a wonderful old castle. It's magical. The mountains hide it, so few people know it's there . . .
	Int:	Thanks for talking to us, Harry . . .
	Harry:	Thank you.

[Pause]

Now listen again.

[The recording is repeated]

[Pause]

That is the end of Part 2.

[Pause]

Now turn to Part 3, questions 14 to 19.

PART 3   *You will hear a man telling some young people about a four-week study programme in a college.*

For each question, fill in the missing information in the numbered space.

You now have 20 seconds to look at Part 3.

[Pause]

Now we are ready to start. Listen carefully. You will hear the recording twice.

Man: If you want to study an interesting subject this summer, and improve your English at the same time, Highbury College is offering three very good courses. As is always the case, each course lasts four weeks. There is an English Literature course, which will deal with 20th-century writers and poets. There is also a course about 18th-century artists, which includes guided tours of the best galleries, and finally a course in Modern Architecture, with visits to some of the city's most famous buildings.

All the courses begin on the 14th of June and the last day of classes is the 12th of July. Classes are from 9 to 3.30, leaving you plenty of time for other activities in the long summer evenings. Fridays are also free for you to have a break because there are lessons on Saturdays and Sundays, too.

Now, about prices. The full price of each course is £425, but the college is offering special discounts for groups. The secretary has further details on that if you are interested. The price includes your accommodation at the college hall – in shared rooms – all meals, full use of the library, and social activities, such as parties, outings, etc . . . Oh, I almost forgot, all books are included too, so you won't have to spend anything on that. But if you need extra lessons, then you have to pay a fee. And you have to make your own travel arrangements to the college.

All the courses are for beginners, so you don't need any previous knowledge of these subjects. Your English should be at a good level, of course, good enough to follow the lectures. If you are interested, see the college secretary, he'll be able to give you copies of the registration forms and the timetable for the course you want.

So, does anyone have any questions?

[Pause]

Now listen again.

[The recording is repeated]

[Pause]

That is the end of Part 3.

[Pause]

Now turn to Part 4, questions 20 to 25.

PART 4 *Look at the six sentences for this part.*

You will hear a conversation between a girl, Claire, and a boy, Tom, about a football tour.

Decide if each sentence is correct or incorrect. If it is correct, put a tick in the box under A for YES. If it is not correct, put a tick in the box under B for NO.

You now have 20 seconds to look at the questions for Part 4.

[Pause]

Now we are ready to start. Listen carefully. You will hear the recording twice.

Tom:	Hello, Claire! I read about you and the women's football team in the daily paper. You must be very pleased about being chosen to go on their national tour this summer.
Claire:	Thanks, Tom. I didn't realise it was in the paper.
Tom:	It says the other girls in the team are all a lot older – does that make you feel nervous?
Claire:	I'm used to it – when I joined our local club, I was only 14 and all the others were in their twenties – but the senior players were very helpful and gave me lots of advice. Now I'm a bit older I can help the other new players when they join.
Tom:	But what about your schoolwork? Isn't it difficult to fit it in? When I was in that tennis team, I never got my homework done on time because I had to do so much practising. That's why I gave it up.
Claire:	Really? Football's not too bad. The matches are all at weekends and we train two evenings a week, so there's still plenty of time for homework.
Tom:	But aren't you planning to go to university when you leave school next year?
Claire:	Well, it's possible to study sports science of course, and I'd like to do that one day. But I think I'll probably concentrate on my football career first, so that's what I'll do next year.
Tom:	I suppose you'd like to play for your country one day?
Claire:	Maybe! At the moment I'm just looking forward to playing against the different teams on this tour. Even if we don't win every game, it'll still be a great experience!
Tom:	By the way – when's your next match?
Claire:	On Saturday afternoon – please come and cheer us on, Tom! We're playing a team that's coming from Manchester.
Tom:	Well, I was born in Manchester, you know! But don't worry. I won't miss the match, and I won't be shouting for the other side either.

[Pause]

Now listen again.

[The recording is repeated]

[Pause]

That is the end of Part 4.

[Pause]

You now have six minutes to check and copy your answers onto the answer sheet.

Note: Teacher, stop the recording here and time six minutes. Remind students when there is **one** minute remaining.

That is the end of the test.

135

Key

Test 3

PAPER 1   READING AND WRITING

READING

Part 1
1 C   2 B   3 A   4 C   5 C

Part 2
6 E   7 G   8 C   9 D   10 B

Part 3
11 A   12 B   13 A   14 B   15 A   16 A   17 B   18 A   19 A   20 B

Part 4
21 C   22 A   23 C   24 D   25 B

Part 5
26 D   27 B   28 C   29 D   30 A   31 B   32 C   33 C   34 D   35 C

WRITING

Part 1
1 gave him/gave my father
2 hasn't/has not/'s not
3 to take/have/get/do/attend
   better take/have/get/do/attend
4 old enough
5 as/so easy/simple

Part 2
Task-specific Mark Scheme
The content elements that need to be covered are:

i   **expression** of thanks (for help)
ii **description** of most useful information
iii **information** about teacher's response to candidate's homework.

The following sample answers can be used as a guide when marking.

SAMPLE A (Test 3, Question 6: Email to a friend)

> Hi Judy,
> Thank you for your information about Britain. You know Britain very well, I think. My teacher was so surprised, because it was such a fantastic homework project. The information about the Queen was the most usefull.
> I hope you write back later.
> Bruno

Examiner Comments

All three parts of the message are clearly communicated.

Mark: 5

SAMPLE B (Test 3, Question 6: Email to a friend)

> Hi Judy.
>
> How are you?
>
> I am thanks a lot for gave me some information about my homework. Your letter gave me some idea about life in Britain.
> I thank life in Britain is very nice, the weather is very nice in the summer also the people very frindly. My teacher gave me good mark.
>
> Thank you
>
> Keep in touch.
>
> Karim

Examiner Comments

Points 1 and 3 are communicated, but point 2 is unclear.

Mark: 3

Key

SAMPLE C (Test 3, Question 6: Email to a friend)

> Hi Judy,
> Thank you about wich you sened me for help.
> I prever how I chooes friendes for my life it is very useful for me. My teacher syed your project very good and keep thes in your life.
> By your Dear Nadir

Examiner Comments

Point 1 is communicated, but points 2 and 3 are irrelevant and unclear.

Mark: 2

SAMPLE D (Test 3, Question 7: Letter to a friend)

> DEAR SUE,
>
> THANK YOU FOR YOUR LETTER.
>
> REGARDING THE QUESTION YOU ASKED ME ABOUT TV IN MY COUNTRY, I HAVE TO SAY THAT I AM NOT REALLY ADDICTED TO WATCHING PROGRAMMES. THE ONLY THING I AM LOOKING FORWARD TO WATCHING IS THE WORLD CUP IN FOOTBALL THAT IS GOING TO START ON NEXT FRIDAY. HOWEVER, IN MY COUNTRY THE MAJORITY OF PEOPLE WATCH TV REGULARLY. VERY POPULAR ARE SOAP OPEARAS AND SHOWS ABOUT PROPERTIES. PEOPLE FIND IT INTERESTING TO WATCH THESE SERIES, ALTHOUGH THEY SEEM TO BE RUNNING FOREVER WITHOUT ANYTHING SPECIAL HAPPENING.
>
> SPEAK TO YOU SOON.
>
> KIND REGARDS
>
> MAREK

Scales	Mark	Commentary
Content	5	All content is relevant and expanded appropriately. The target reader is fully informed.
Communicative Achievement	5	The letter format is appropriate and the letter holds the reader's attention throughout. Although the register is slightly formal, it is consistent.
Organisation	5	The letter is generally well-organised and with good internal cohesion. A range of cohesive devices is used appropriately (Regarding *the question you asked me*; However, *in my country*; People find it interesting to watch these *series*, although *they seem*). There is good internal cohesion.
Language	5	A good range of everyday and less common lexis is used appropriately (*addicted to; the majority of people; soap opearas and shows about properties; running forever*). A range of simple and some complex grammatical forms (relative clauses, use of gerund and infinitive forms, range of tenses) are used with a good degree of control. Errors are minimal.

Key

SAMPLE E (Test 3, Question 7: Letter to a friend)

> Dear Sue,
>
> It's great to know from you, tell me about your family and how your boyfriend Mat?
>
> I think in Venezuela people are not really interested in TV programmes actually children are who watch them unless it's news time maybe news are the most famous programmes adults are always watching the news.
>
> There are lots of TV programmes like who wants to be a millionare which so interesting, of course there are movies but they aren't really good. We watch most of the American series. Dramas and comedies are quite good.
>
> I always enjoy watching Friends, the news and some cartoons, I love Tom and Jerry. There are few reallity shows but I don't like them.
>
> I'm looking forward to hearing from you.
>
> love Sophia

Scales	Mark	Commentary
Content	5	All elements of the task are covered with appropriate expansion. The target reader is fully informed.
Communicative Achievement	5	The conventions of letter writing are used to hold the reader's attention and communicate ideas effectively. Register and format are consistently appropriate.
Organisation	4	The text is generally well-organised and coherent, using suitable paragraphing. A limited number of linking words (*and; but*) and some cohesive devices (*unless; which so interesting; I don't like* them) are used. However, a lack of punctuation affects the coherence at times, particularly in the second paragraph.
Language	4	A range of everyday vocabulary is used appropriately, with some evidence of less common lexis appropriate to the task (*cartoons; Dramas and comedies; reallity shows*). Simple grammatical forms (mainly limited to the present simple tense) are used with a good degree of control. Some non-impeding errors are present.

SAMPLE F (Test 3, Question 7: Letter to a friend)

> In my country TV is good for watch becaze you can use for sport or news or film when I'm in my country evry night befor go to bed I watch the TV football or karate or film or news now I'm in england I cant wach becaze I don't have free time I most to estady in my country my mom or m sister. They are watch TV too much They are watching just film my mother never watch the sport she don't like and my favrert porogram karate sport becaze I love sport. sport for body is very good.

Scales	Mark	Commentary
Content	4	The task is addressed but there is limited information about TV habits in the candidate's own country. The target reader is informed.
Communicative Achievement	3	The conventions of the communicative task are used in generally appropriate ways to communicate straightforward ideas. Register is appropriate, but letter format has not been used. The target reader has to work hard to follow the message.
Organisation	2	The text is connected using basic, high-frequency linking words (*becaze; and*) and a limited number of cohesive devices (*They are watch TV; she don't like*). Lack of punctuation and paragraphing cause some difficulty for the target reader.
Language	2	Basic vocabulary is used appropriately. Errors are mainly with spelling and do not affect communication (*becaze; evry; wach; favrert*). Simple grammatical forms are used with some degree of control, but there are a number of distracting errors (*They are watching just film; my favrert porogram karate sport; sport for body is very good*), some of which may obscure the message (*I most to estady*).

Key

SAMPLE G (Test 3, Question 8: Story)

> I looked in the shop window and I saw exactly what I wanted. It was the brandnew 'Mac Book pro', I really wanted it but I didn't have enough money for it, so I had to wait until I had enough money but that could take a while because I only got £5 pocket money per week. That really annoyed me. All day I thought: "How can I get the money for the computer?" And then it came to me. I went to my mother and asked her: "Mom, could you lend me some money for a computer?" She answered: 'Yes but I want it back!" So I bought the computer.

Scales	Mark	Commentary
Content	5	The story continues naturally from the prompt sentence and the target reader would be able to follow the storyline with no problems.
Communicative Achievement	5	Ideas are communicated effectively following the conventions of storytelling and a consistently appropriate register and format are used, holding the target reader's attention throughout.
Organisation	5	The text is well-organised and coherent, using a variety of linking words and cohesive devices with flexibility (*I really wanted* it *but I didn't have enough money . . . so I had to wait* until *I had enough money* but that *could take a while because ...;* That *really annoyed me;* And then it *came to me; Yes but I want* it *back!*).
Language	5	A range of everyday and more complex vocabulary is used appropriately (*brandnew; pocket money; it came to me*). A range of simple and some more complex grammatical forms (i.e. narrative tenses; relative clauses and the well-controlled second sentence) are used with good control.

SAMPLE H (Test 3, Question 8: Story)

I looked in the shop window and I saw exactly what I wanted. After one week looking for this T-Shirt I found It by luck. I was so happy. I felt that my heart is jumping. I pushed the door hardly and it made a lot of nois, All of the costomers was looking at me 'sorry' I said. But no-one gaves me attintion.

I went to the slales man and I asked him about the T-shirt, But he answerd me with a cold heart "they are sold out". ooh man I didn't felt anything for five minutes. I get out feeling so down. It's my best friend birthday. And he really want this. I was walking thinking what can I get untill I saw a small shop selling them, I am so lucky. I bought five t-shirts with all kind of the colors and I went home.

Scales	Mark	Commentary
Content	5	The story continues from the prompt sentence and the target reader would be able to follow the storyline with no problems.
Communicative Achievement	4	Register and story format are appropriate. Ideas are generally communicated clearly, although some effort is required at the end of the first paragraph.
Organisation	3	Although inappropriate punctuation and short sentences distract at times, the text is connected and largely coherent. Basic linking words (*After; but; and*) and a limited number of cohesive devices (*I found It by luck; I pushed the door ... and it made a lot of nois; I saw a small shop selling them*) are used.
Language	3	A range of everyday vocabulary is used and some less common lexis (*my heart is jumping; with a cold heart; sold out; feeling so down*) is used. A number of errors are present (*I pushed the door hardly; nois; costomers; attintion; slales man*) but they do not impede communication. Simple grammatical forms are used with reasonable control, although there are inconsistencies with the use of past tenses and subject/verb agreement.

Key

SAMPLE I (Test 3, Question 8: Story)

> I looked in the shop window and I saw exactly what I wanted. Than something speily was waiting for. It was a car. A sport car. That car was so nice. But to expence. I don't have much cash to buy. Because my card was let in my home. So I got a good idea at that moment. I got in that shop and see around. There were no people next to that car. So I went to that car. When I got in the car. Something was lock. I have to stay in the car. I can't went out any more.
>
> At last. I never go out the car. So I am a car. Car is me.

Scales	Mark	Commentary
Content	4	The story continues from the prompt sentence and the target reader is informed, but the message is confused towards the end.
Communicative Achievement	4	Straightforward ideas are communicated using an appropriate register and format. Some effort is required to follow the storyline at times, for example in the second and final sentences.
Organisation	2	The story is connected, but the short sentences and over-use of full stops cause some difficulty for the target reader.
		Basic linking words (*but; because; at that moment; so*) and a limited number of cohesive devices (It *was a car. A sport car;* That *car was so nice*) are used.
Language	2	Everyday vocabulary is used reasonably appropriately, despite some spelling errors (*than; expence*) and incorrect word choices (*let in my home; see around*).
		Simple grammatical forms are used with reasonable control, although there are frequent problems with past tenses.
		Errors are noticeable and may distract and impede meaning at times (*Than something speily was waiting for; At last. I never go out the car*).

PAPER 2 LISTENING

Part 1
1 C   2 A   3 C   4 A   5 A   6 C   7 B

Part 2
8 A   9 B   10 B   11 C   12 B   13 C

Part 3
14 1921
    Nineteen (hundred) (and) twenty(-)one
    One thousand, nine hundred and twenty(-)one
15 Japan(ese)
16 gift(s)
17 hotel (next door)
18 (rail/railway/train) station
19 group(s)

Part 4
20 B   21 A   22 B   23 B   24 B   25 A

Key

Test 3 transcript

This is the Cambridge Preliminary English Test, Test 3. There are four parts to the test. You will hear each part twice. For each part of the test there will be time for you to look through the questions and time for you to check your answers.

Write your answers on the question paper. You will have six minutes at the end of the test to copy your answers onto the answer sheet.

The recording will now be stopped. Please ask any questions now, because you must not speak during the test.

[Pause]

Now open your question paper and look at Part 1.

[Pause]

PART 1

There are seven questions in this part. For each question there are three pictures and a short recording. Choose the correct picture and put a tick in the box below it.

Before we start, here is an example.

Where did the man leave his camera?

Man:	Oh, no! I haven't got my camera!
Woman:	But you used it just now to take a photograph of the fountain.
Man:	Oh, I remember, I put it down on the steps while I put my coat on.
Woman:	Well, let's drive back quickly – it might still be there.

[Pause]

The first picture is correct so there is a tick in box A.

Look at the three pictures for question 1 now.

[Pause]

Now we are ready to start. Listen carefully. You will hear each recording twice.

One. Which present will the girl receive?

Mum:	What would you like for your birthday, Maria? Would you like a new carpet for your bedroom floor? Your room's quite dark – it would really make it brighter in there . . .
Maria:	Mmm . . . well, I did see a wonderful collection of short stories in a shop yesterday. I'd really like that. And don't forget I'm going on holiday soon – a really nice leather suitcase would be great.
Mum:	Oh, dear. I was sure you'd really love my idea, so I'm afraid I've already got it . . .
Maria:	Oh, Mum!

[Pause]

Now listen again.

[The recording is repeated]

[Pause]

Two. Where will the tourists go last?

Guide:	I hope you're all enjoying this walking tour of Kingston. We've visited the oldest building in the city – the castle. We still have the famous gardens to see and the trip on the river boat which we're going to do at the end of the day. But next I suggest that we have a break for lunch here in the town park. There's a café just over there and plenty of seats as well . . .

[Pause]

Now listen again.

[The recording is repeated]

[Pause]

146

Three. How much does the man pay for the postage?

Man: I'd like to send a parcel to Hong Kong please. How much will it cost?

Woman: I'll need to weigh it before I can tell you . . . Okay . . . If you send this by air, which is more expensive than by sea, it'll be 18 euros and 50 cents. By sea, it'll be about half that . . . erm . . . 7 euros 50 cents.

Man: I need to send it by air, so I'll pay the extra. But last time, I think I only paid 15 euros 50 cents for the same weight! Have prices increased?

Woman: Yes. Sorry!

[Pause]

Now listen again.

[The recording is repeated]

[Pause]

Four. Where in the theatre did the woman leave her gloves?

Woman: Good morning, I lost a pair of black leather gloves at the theatre last night, but I'm not sure where. I know I kept them with me when I left my coat in the cloakroom.

Man: We have found a pair this morning, under one of the seats.

Woman: Oh, now I remember! I put them on my seat when I went to the coffee bar during the interval. They probably fell on the floor when I came back.

Man: Well, you can collect them from the ticket office any time.

[Pause]

Now listen again.

[The recording is repeated]

[Pause]

Five. Which dress does the woman like best?

Woman: Ooh look . . . that dress with the spots is really nice. Shall I buy it?

Man: Hmm, it's a bit expensive, though it would look really good on you. But that white one is really nice. You always look great in white. This one with the flowers would look good on you too, and look – it's half price!

Woman: I'm not very keen on that material. And I prefer the spotty one to the white one, don't you?

Man: Oh, well, it's better if you decide which one you want.

[Pause]

Now listen again.

[The recording is repeated]

[Pause]

Six. What is the television programme about?

Maria: Hi, Daniella. It's Maria. There's a really good programme you might like to watch on TV tonight – at nine. That presenter you like, the woman who films elephants in Africa – she's doing a special programme.

Daniella: Is she going back to Africa?

Maria: Well, this time she's visiting the South Pole, to study some of the wildlife there. It looks like they had a difficult time making the programme. The weather was so bad, they couldn't fly there . . . it took two weeks just to get there by ship.

Daniella: That'll be interesting, thanks!

[Pause]

Now listen again.

147

Key

[*The recording is repeated*]

[Pause]

Seven. Which vehicle does Steve intend to buy?

Man: I saw Steve's wife driving his sports car the other day.

Woman: Did you? He told me he was going to sell it because with three children he needs to get something more practical – you know, a four-door car with lots of space for luggage.

Man: Well, he's got a van which he uses for his business, but I suppose he can't really put the children in the back of that. I might think of buying that sports car, actually.

Woman: Really?

[Pause]

Now listen again.

[The recording is repeated]

[Pause]

That is the end of Part 1.

[Pause]

PART 2 *Now turn to Part 2, questions 8 to 13.*

You will hear part of a radio interview with a woman called Linda Brown, who is talking about working in a cake shop when she was a student.

For each question, put a tick in the correct box.

You now have 45 seconds to look at the questions for Part 2.

[Pause]

Now we are ready to start. Listen carefully. You will hear the recording twice.

Int: Now Linda, let's talk about your first job.

Linda: Well, I was an assistant in an expensive cake shop in the small town where I lived. It was my last year at school, before I went to college. I wanted to earn extra money for myself because I come from a family of seven and my parents couldn't afford to give us much pocket money.

Int: Did you like your first boss?

Linda: He was always polite, never shouted at us, even when we dropped things; and that was good for a young girl like me who wasn't very confident. He knew everything about the business. I had no proper training, but it was good experience working for someone with so much knowledge. He didn't pay us well, but I didn't expect to earn much in my first job.

Int: And what about the shop? Was it a nice place to work?

Linda: As I say, it was an expensive shop, and the cakes were beautiful. Then in the morning there was this wonderful smell of bread baking. The first week was difficult because I just wanted to eat the cakes, which wasn't allowed, but then I lost interest in them. We had to keep everything clean, and that was hard work.

Int: Did you do any of the baking yourself?

Linda: There were two chefs who were specialists in making cakes for celebrations, and creating new bread recipes. I loved watching them at work, but I wasn't allowed to touch the ones on display in the windows. We sold sandwiches at lunchtime – again, very luxurious ones, and the shop assistants had to make those. I learnt to put in really generous fillings, much more than I used at home.

Int: How did you get on with the other shop assistants?

Linda: One of them was my best friend, which was great, but the full-time staff sometimes treated us like silly schoolgirls because we couldn't cook. But I was surprised

	because the full-time assistants couldn't add up in their head. I was good at it, but they used calculators if there was anything difficult to work out.
Int:	Did you enjoy serving customers in the shop?
Linda:	The best part of the day was lunchtime, when we were busy. Time just flew. Then it was interesting when people came in to plan a party or a wedding. One of the chefs would come through to discuss the design of the cake. Some customers thought the prices were too high, but usually ended up buying the cakes anyway.

[Pause]

Now listen again.

[The recording is repeated]

[Pause]

That is the end of Part 2.

[Pause]

PART 3 *Now turn to Part 3, questions 14 to 19.*

You will hear some recorded information about a museum.

For each question, fill in the missing information in the numbered space.

You now have 20 seconds to look at Part 3.

[Pause]

Now we are ready to start. Listen carefully. You will hear the recording twice.

Man:	Thank you for calling the Central Museum information line.
	Central Museum is open every day from 2nd January through to 31st December and is open daily from 10 am until 5 pm. The museum itself is a wonderful example of local architecture, completed in the year 1889, and the gardens, still in their original 1921 design, surprise and delight visitors of all ages.
	The museum contains an important 19th-century English furniture collection as well as a permanent Japanese art exhibition and admission is free to all visitors. Admission includes a free pre-recorded audio guide and we are fully equipped to welcome wheelchair users.
	Our museum shop sells a variety of books, cards and gifts. You'll find all kinds of interesting ideas for both adults and children. The museum also has a café, offering a selection of hot and cold dishes throughout the day from 10 until 4 30.
	For visitors travelling by car, parking is available at the hotel next door. It's just metres away from the museum. There is also frequent local public transport with buses to and from the town centre. There are also buses from the railway station every ten minutes throughout the day.
	For further information about the museum, its history and its collections, please call 01202 451800. You can also call 451858 for information about group visits, or if you're interested in hiring a room at the museum. Teachers can look at our website on www.centralmuseum.uk where they'll find lots of ideas for project work. Thank you for calling the Central Museum information line.

[Pause]

Now listen again.

[The recording is repeated]

[Pause]

That is the end of Part 3.

[Pause]

Key

PART 4　　*Now turn to Part 4, questions 20 to 25.*

Look at the six sentences for this part. You will hear a conversation between a boy, Sam, and a girl, Carla, about a school concert.

Decide if each sentence is correct or incorrect. If it is correct, put a tick in the box under A for YES. If it is not correct, put a tick in the box under B for NO.

You now have 20 seconds to look at the questions for Part 4.

[Pause]

Now we are ready to start. Listen carefully. You will hear the recording twice.

Sam: Carla . . .

Carla: What is it, Sam?

Sam: Why weren't you at Mrs Ford's meeting this morning? The one about the school concert?

Carla: Well, I've decided not to take part this year.

Sam: You're joking! The whole orchestra wondered where you were and Mrs Ford even sent someone to look for you.

Carla: I already know about that! What it is to be popular . . .

Sam: Everyone's expecting you to do the concert, you know. And Mrs Ford has found some music for you.

Carla: But that's the problem, Sam. We're never allowed to select what we play . . . and her choices are so boring!

Sam: Oh, that's a bit unfair. I agree that it used to be like that, but the programme she put together for last year's concert was much better. You enjoyed it last year, didn't you?

Carla: Well, the event itself was great and I was proud of how I played, but it's always such hard work getting ready for that, all those hours practising. And I don't have so much time to spare this year.

Sam: I suppose not . . . But Carla, we really need you. Apart from David in class 10, who's brilliant, nobody else plays the piano as well as you do. And David's going to be away that week.

Carla: Oh, do you want me to feel guilty now? Well, when's the first practice?

Sam: Thursday lunchtime. Look, if you don't like the music Mrs Ford's decided on, why not say so!

Carla: And suggest something else?

Sam: Well, you'll be playing the piece on your own, won't you, so why not?

Carla: That's true . . . anyway, what about you, Sam? Aren't you busy at the moment?

Sam: Yeah, there's lots of course work and I'm playing in the school football team! You're right, I'll have to give something up, won't I? But not the concert, that's for sure.

Carla: Well, good for you. Okay, I'll see you on Thursday then!

Sam: Excellent!

[Pause]

Now listen again.

[The recording is repeated]

[Pause]

That is the end of Part 4.

[Pause]

You now have six minutes to check and copy your answers onto the answer sheet.

Note: Teacher, stop the recording here and time six minutes. Remind students when there is **one** minute remaining

That is the end of the test.

Test 4

PAPER 1 READING AND WRITING

READING

Part 1
1 C   2 C   3 A   4 A   5 B

Part 2
6 F   7 C   8 H   9 D   10 B

Part 3
11 B   12 A   13 B   14 B   15 A   16 B   17 B   18 A   19 A   20 A

Part 4
21 C   22 C   23 B   24 A   25 D

Part 5
26 D   27 B   28 B   29 A   30 C   31 D   32 A   33 D   34 C   35 B

WRITING

Part 1
1 less
2 I would/I'd
3 difficult/hard (at all)
4 learn/find out/discover/teach yourself/be taught
5 during

Part 2

Task-specific Mark Scheme

The content elements that need to be covered are:

i **information** about what new clothes candidate bought
ii **reference** to where candidate bought clothes
iii **reason** why candidate needed to buy these clothes.

The following sample answers can be used as a guide when marking.

Key

SAMPLE A (Test 4, Question 6: Email to a friend)

> Hi Alex!
>
> Guess what? I went shopping last weekend! I went with Claire to Walmart because next Friday I'm having my first job interview. She help to choose what kind of trousers or skirts I could wear and also I bought a white blouse.
>
> See you soon
>
> Cristina

Examiner Comments

All three parts of the message are clearly communicated.

Mark: 5

SAMPLE B (Test 4, Question 6: Email to a friend)

> Dear Alex
> Today I'm very happy because I bought some new clothes In fact I went out and I went to the city center this morning I bought a shoes that I'll dress tomorrow, and I bought something for you What about do you come me so you can take the surprace?
> love Eva

Examiner Comments

Points 1 and 2 are communicated, but point 3 has not been attempted.

Mark: 3

SAMPLE C (Test 4, Question 6: Email to a friend)

> Alex
>
> Hello I am Julieta, can you tell me, yesterday I was see you, and I could see a T-shirt, and where are you bought the clothes from? because tomorrow is the birthday of Sergio, I need buy him gif, what clothes I can buy?
>
> bye Julieta

Examiner Comments

Only the third point has been communicated, although the second point has been attempted.

Mark: 2

Key

SAMPLE D (Test 4, Question 7: Letter to a friend)

> Hi John, I don't mind crowded place because I like to be in a crowd. My home is in a quite street near Tooting Broadway station and even if it is little busy, my street isn't.
> In there live a lot of people but almost of them move by tube so there isn't so much trafic on roads. The only problem is that Clapham is on the way to go home and it is very busy so, it takes too long to go home from the city center. If I were able to move I would live in Stockwell because it's quite near to the city center.
> It is also a good place without too many social problems and I'd like to live there, it's confortable for me.
> See you soon, Michael

Scales	Mark	Commentary
Content	5	All content is relevant to the task and appropriately expanded. The target reader is fully informed.
Communicative Achievement	5	The letter holds the reader's attention throughout, using the appropriate register and format for the task.
Organisation	5	The text is well-organised and coherent, using a reasonable variety of linking words (*because; and; so*) and cohesive devices (*almost of* them; *The only problem is* that; it's *quite near to the city center*; *I'd like to live* there). Use of paragraphing is appropriate and there is good internal cohesion within and across long sentences.
Language	4	A range of everyday and some less common (*crowded; social problems*) vocabulary are used appropriately. There are several spelling errors, but they do not impede communication. A range of simple grammatical forms is used with reasonable control. There is also some evidence of more complex grammatical forms (e.g. use of the second conditional at the end of the second paragraph). Some non-impeding errors of structure and vocabulary are present (*My home is in a quite street; In there live a lot of people; almost of them move by tube; it's confortable for me*).

SAMPLE E (Test 4, Question 7: Letter to a friend)

> Hi!
>
> In my case, I live in a very quiet street, there is sometimes a little bit of noise at the weekends, but it's okay. In my street and around my place aren't live too many people so for that reason is quiet. That thing changes if you go to the city centre all busy, a lot of people and too much traffic.
>
> Anyway I like to live in places not busy and not loudly. If I had the option to move I would like to move in a very quiet place in a mountainous place. For example, the north of Spain will be a fantastic place for me to live in.
>
> Antonio

Scales	Mark	Commentary
Content	5	All content is relevant and expanded appropriately. The target reader is fully informed.
Communicative Achievement	5	A consistently appropriate informal register and format are used. The letter holds the reader's attention and ideas are communicated effectively.
Organisation	4	The text is coherent and generally well-organised, using a reasonable range of linking words (*but; so; for example*) and cohesive devices (*there is sometimes a little bit of noise ... but it's okay; so for that reason; Anyway*).
Language	4	A range of everyday vocabulary is used appropriately, with limited examples of more complex lexis (*mountainous; the option to move*). Simple grammatical forms are used with reasonable control, although there are instances of poor control at sentence level (*In my street ... aren't live too many people; if you go to the city centre all busy; for that reason is quiet; I like to live in places not busy and not loudly*). There is some evidence of more complex grammatical forms (*If I had the option to move I would like to move; The north of Spain will be a fantastic place for me to live in*). Some non-impeding errors are present.

Key

SAMPLE F (Test 4, Question 7: Letter to a friend)

> My name Mazhar I leave in London near Oxford Street this street so buisy and noisy. I can't sleep at night I want to chang my flat to sababce. I work very hard and keep my money to change I wan to buy detachet house with little, garden that this house inclued indopool, five bedroons, two tolites, one kichen, siting-room and one big sport hole. I like do sport every morning.

Scales	Mark	Commentary
Content	4	The task is addressed and the target reader is informed, although there is limited expansion.
Communicative Achievement	3	Straightforward ideas are communicated. Register is appropriate but there is no attempt at a letter format. The reader has to work hard to follow the message at times, for example in the third long sentence.
Organisation	1	The text is connected using only a very limited range of basic linking words and cohesive devices (*and; this street*). There is a lack of control of punctuation, for example in the sentence beginning *I work very hard*, which causes confusion for the target reader.
Language	2	Everyday vocabulary is used with frequent errors of spelling, some of which distract and may impede communication at times (*leave in London; buisy; sababce; tolites; sport hole*). Simple grammatical forms, limited to the present tense, are used with some degree of control. A number of errors are present, but meaning can largely be determined.

SAMPLE G (Test 4, Question 8: Story)

> **AN UNUSUAL REQUEST**
>
> I was in my bedroom when I saw something out of the window. I was sure I saw something black so I went close to the window just to have a look outside. I didn't see anything so I came back to my bed and I started again to read a book.
>
> My mother came into my room just to ask me if I had seen something arownd the house.
>
> When she left my room I heard a voice from the window asking me if I wanted a mouse to eat. It was so unusual because the speaker was a black cat.

Scales	Mark	Commentary
Content	5	The story is clearly related to the title. The target reader would be fully informed.
Communicative Achievement	5	The story flows well and holds the reader's attention throughout, using a consistently appropriate register and format.
Organisation	5	The text is well-organised and coherent. There is effective use of linking words (*when; so; because*) and cohesive devices (*My mother came into my room just to ask me; When she left my room I heard a voice ... asking me if I wanted a mouse to eat. It was so unusual because the speaker was a black cat*). There is good cohesion within and across sentences and effective use of paragraphing.
Language	5	A range of everyday lexis is used appropriately, with some evidence of more complex vocabulary (*something black; have a look outside*). Simple and some complex grammatical forms (*to ask me if I had seen; I heard a voice ... asking me if I wanted a mouse to eat*) are used with good control. Errors are minimal and do not impede communication.

Key

SAMPLE H (Test 4, Question 8: Story)

AN UNUSUAL REQUEST

Yesterday I was walking on the street, as Tom, my best friend, asked me: "Do you have 100 dollars?" I was really surprised. He never asked me moneys! "Why do you need them?" I asked. "That's not important!" he answered me. I never saw him so serious. Fortunately I had this moneys, and I gave them to him. As I put them in his hands, he runned away as fast as he could, but I followed him. He arrived in a dark street, where a man was waiting for him.
My best friend was taking drugs, and I had to help him.

Scales	Mark	Commentary
Content	5	The story is clearly linked to the title and the target reader is fully informed.
Communicative Achievement	5	The story flows well and holds the reader's attention right to the end. Register and format are appropriate.
Organisation	5	The text is generally well-organised and coherent, using some linking words (*and; but*) and a good range of cohesive devices (*I was walking on the street, as Tom, my best friend, asked me; Fortunately, I had this moneys, and I gave them to him; As I put them in his hands, he runned away . . . but I followed him; a dark street, where a man was waiting*). Although there is limited paragraphing, internal cohesion is good.
Language	4	A range of everyday vocabulary is used appropriately. A range of simple grammatical forms are used with a good degree of control. There is some evidence of more complex structures in the second half of the story (from *As I put them in his hands ...*) Some errors are present, mainly with uncountable forms and tenses (*He never asked me moneys!; I never saw him so serious; 'he runned away*) but they do not impede communication.

158

SAMPLE I (Test 4, Question 8: Story)

> AN UNUSUAL REQUEST
>
> I'm staing in the park whit Amy, my best friend and we taking to her boyfriend; often, my friend Amy talk about he. I think that she loved so mach this boy; but, at the moment he are studing in England. While I and Amy are walking she say me to meet her boyfriend Mark when he retourn. I think now that it is an unusual request.

Scales	Mark	Commentary
Content	4	The candidate has made a clear attempt at linking the story to the title, but the text is not fully developed. The target reader is informed. However, more information is needed to fully understand the story.
Communicative Achievement	2	Register and format are appropriate. Ideas are communicated, but the target reader has to work hard at times to follow the storyline, due to the number of errors (*we taking to her boyfriend*).
Organisation	3	The text is connected and coherent, using basic linking words (*and; often; but; when*) and some cohesive devices (*this boy; at the moment; While I and Amy are walking; when he retourn*).
Language	2	In general, everyday vocabulary is used appropriately, but there are a number of distracting spelling errors (*staing; whit; taking to her boyfriend; mach*). Simple grammatical forms are used with some degree of control. A number of errors are present, particularly with tenses and verb forms, but meaning can still be determined (*Amy talk about he; she loved so mach this boy; he are studing in England*).

Key

PAPER 2 LISTENING

Part 1
1 B   2 B   3 C   4 A   5 A   6 B   7 C

Part 2
8 A   9 C   10 B   11 C   12 C   13 A

Part 3
14 Good Living
15 fish/fishes
16 salad(s)
17 rice(s)
18 parties/party
19 (£)2.49/two (pound(s)) (and) forty(-)nine (p/pence)

Part 4
20 B   21 A   22 A   23 B   24 B   25 B

Test 4

Test 4 transcript

This is the Cambridge Preliminary English Test, Test 4. There are four parts to the test. You will hear each part twice. For each part of the test there will be time for you to look through the questions and time for you to check your answers.

Write your answers on the question paper. You will have six minutes at the end of the test to copy your answers onto the answer sheet.

The recording will now be stopped. Please ask any questions now, because you must not speak during the test.

[Pause]

Now open your question paper and look at Part 1.

[Pause]

PART 1 *There are seven questions in this part. For each question there are three pictures and a short recording. Choose the correct picture and put a tick in the box below it.*

Before we start, here is an example.

Where did the man leave his camera?

Man:	Oh, no! I haven't got my camera!
Woman:	But you used it just now to take a photograph of the fountain.
Man:	Oh, I remember, I put it down on the steps while I put my coat on.
Woman:	Well, let's drive back quickly – it might still be there.

[Pause]

The first picture is correct so there is a tick in box A.

Look at the three pictures for question 1 now.

[Pause]

Now we are ready to start. Listen carefully. You will hear each recording twice.

One. Which prize has the man just won?

Int:	And in second place, Tim Davidson. Tim, would you like to say a few words?
Tim:	Well, I want to thank everyone who has helped me to do so well today, because it's not just about me the player, there's my trainer, my manager, and my wife Jane. I know she'll love this beautiful glass bowl, so it won't be up on a dusty shelf with the cups I've won in the past. We'll enjoy looking at it every day. And I'll be back next year to win that silver plate! Thank you.

[Pause]

Now listen again.

[The recording is repeated]

[Pause]

Two. What was the man's first job?

Man:	I know you think being a postman's not a very good job – long hours and not a lot of money – but I enjoy it. Better than some things I've done. When I first left school I spent a month or two cleaning windows, and then I got a job building houses. Now that was hard! Of course, when I was at school, I dreamt of becoming a pilot, but I failed to get on a training course.

[Pause]

Now listen again.

161

Key

[The recording is repeated]

[Pause]

Three. Where will they have something to eat?

Girl: I'm really hungry. Can we stop for something to eat before we get to the airport?

Man: Sorry, there isn't enough time to stop at a café. Your mother's flight gets in at ten o'clock, and we've still got quite a long way to go. We don't want to keep her waiting, so I think we'll go straight to the airport. We'll need petrol on the way home, so we can stop for a snack at a service station.

[Pause]

Now listen again.

[The recording is repeated]

[Pause]

Four. What does the woman's house look like now?

Woman: It was really strange going back to Redmond, where I used to live. Everything has changed so much. I went to see my old house. It used to have trees in the garden and a hedge in the front. Well, the people who own it now have built another bedroom over the top of the garage, and removed the trees and hedge so they have more room to park their cars. It made me feel really sad, because it looked so different.

[Pause]

Now listen again.

[The recording is repeated]

[Pause]

Five. Which sport will they do tomorrow?

Boy: It's great here. I've just been horse-riding for the first time in my life, and tomorrow I'm going to learn how to dive off the high board in the swimming pool. I had no idea there were so many things available.

Girl: No, I came for the cycling mainly, so I haven't tried all the other things. To be honest, I don't think the pool is for me really, although I'd like to try the riding. Would you be interested in doing that again tomorrow with me, instead of the diving?

Boy: Yeah, I suppose so.

[Pause]

Now listen again.

[The recording is repeated]

[Pause]

Six. What can you see on the television programme?

Coming up next on The Science Channel is the latest documentary produced and presented by photographer Daniel Hamilton, who made the prize-winning series about African animals which you may have seen last year. His latest series is simply called *Earth*, and viewers can enjoy some amazing photography, with pictures of the planet shot from cameras in space using the latest satellite technology. So sit back, relax and enjoy!

[Pause]

Now listen again.

[The recording is repeated]

Test 4

[Pause]

Seven. Where will the man sit on the plane?

Man: On the plane at last! Now – our seats are in Row 12 . . . over there!

Woman: Yes, A and B. Seat A is next to the window. Do you want that one? Or do you prefer to sit in the middle?

Man: Well, they said the seat on the end seems to be empty too, so I'll take that one instead. I'm not that keen to see outside . . .

Woman: Well, I love looking at the clouds, so I'll sit near the window. We'll put our newspapers in the middle. Okay?

[Pause]

Now listen again.

[The recording is repeated]

[Pause]

That is the end of Part 1.

[Pause]

PART 2 *Now turn to Part 2, questions 8 to 13.*

You will hear an interview with a woman called Lucy Rainbow, who is talking about her job as a painter.

For each question, put a tick in the correct box.

You now have 45 seconds to look at the questions for Part 2.

[Pause]

Now we are ready to start. Listen carefully. You will hear the recording twice.

Int: Today we have with us in the studio Lucy Rainbow, who earns her living as a painter. Good morning, Lucy. Can you tell us about your job?

Lucy: Well, I don't paint pretty pictures you can hang on your walls at home. Mainly, I work in a theatre, painting the background scenery for plays. I've also done a couple of CD covers. That was great, because I got to meet my favourite pop stars.

Int: So how did all this start?

Lucy: Well, I always intended to become a proper artist. But I couldn't sell any of my paintings, and anyway I got bored working alone! I was offered a job in an advertising agency, but the idea of working in a theatre attracted me more. I get the chance to paint something different every day, I get paid reasonably well, and I work with a team of wonderful people.

Int: So you enjoy your work, but doesn't it have any disadvantages?

Lucy: Mostly, I love it. The only thing that causes me stress is that often I have too many things to do at the same time, while at other times I have nothing to do. It's difficult to organise my time, but I always make sure I stop for lunch.

Int: How many hours do you work on an average day?

Lucy: There's no such thing as an average day! But generally, I start work at eight in the morning, and go through until seven. That makes it an eleven-hour day, which is much longer than the eight hours that most people work.

Int: Is your journey to work difficult?

Lucy: Not really. My dream job would be one where I could walk to work, but that hasn't happened yet. I could drive to the theatre, but that makes me tired and I get a lot of my best ideas when I'm on my way to work, on the bus or train.

163

Key

> Int: Do you have time for any hobbies?
>
> Lucy: Not as much as I'd like. I used to play a lot of tennis until I hurt my ankle, and I was a regular visitor to an art gallery near my home until it closed down. In the little spare time I have, I'm doing a course in computer graphics. I hope what I learn will help me in my job.
>
> Int: Well, thank you, Lucy. It's been interesting talking to you.
>
> [Pause]
>
> *Now listen again.*
>
> [The recording is repeated]
>
> *That is the end of Part 2.*
>
> [Pause]

PART 3

Now turn to Part 3, questions 14 to 19.

You will hear a radio announcement about a new magazine.

For each question, fill in the missing information in the numbered space.

You now have 20 seconds to look at Part 3.

[Pause]

Now we are ready to start. Listen carefully. You will hear the recording twice.

Today we begin the programme with some information about an exciting magazine that will be on sale in the shops next week. It's called *Good Living* and the aim of the magazine is to show you how to eat well, and in a healthy way. So every month there will be information about which fruit and vegetables are in season as well as lots of recipes by top chefs for you to make. In the first issue of the magazine, there will be recipes for fish, which is a good choice if you want to eat healthily. In addition, you'll also find a special free gift. This is a DVD showing how to prepare summer salads, using a wide variety of different ingredients, some of them quite unusual.

The second issue will have an interesting article about the history of tea and the many kinds you can buy in different countries. It also has a special collection of recipes for children, which will show them some interesting things to make with rice. Of course, there'll be some good things for adults in this second magazine, too. There are some wonderful recipes designed especially for parties. The recipes are quick to prepare and very colourful, and some can also be made ahead of time and frozen, which is always useful.

Now the price of the magazine will normally be £3.99, but the first issue will be on sale at £2.49, so that's a good offer, a reduction of £1.50. It will be on sale in supermarkets and newsagents on Monday. So make sure you buy it – the ideas and photos in it are great!

Moving on, next on the programme . . .

[Pause]

Now listen again.

[The recording is repeated]

[Pause]

That is the end of Part 3.

[Pause]

PART 4

Now turn to Part 4, questions 20 to 25.

Look at the six sentences for this part. You will hear a man called Karl, and his wife Jenny, talking about the holiday they have just had.

Decide if each sentence is correct or incorrect. If it is correct, put a tick in the box under A for YES. If it is not correct, put a tick in the box under B for NO.

Test 4

You now have 20 seconds to look at the questions for Part 4.

[Pause]

Now we are ready to start. Listen carefully. You will hear the recording twice.

Karl: Phew! Home at last! That journey seemed to last forever. I'm glad to be back, aren't you?

Jenny: Not really. I'm sorry our holiday's over. I'll miss the beach. We had a great time, didn't we?

Karl: Mmm . . . it was okay. The weather wasn't as good as I'd hoped. I thought the forecast was for bright sunshine the whole week!

Jenny: Well, most of the week was like that. We only had a little bit of rain, didn't we? And they did mention that on the forecast.

Karl: Yes, the day after it rained! Anyway, the food in the hotel was delicious, wasn't it?

Jenny: It was, yeah . . .

Karl: And it was good to be able to help ourselves to what we wanted.

Jenny: Mmm . . . it saved delays, and it meant we could get out quickly in the mornings, too. The waiters were very helpful, I must say.

Karl: Mmm . . . that was good.

Jenny: The only thing I wasn't happy about was the temperature in the room. It was so hot!

Karl: It certainly was. It didn't help when we opened the windows, either. It didn't cool it down at all, did it?

Jenny: No. Still, it was just the same when we went to that other hotel last year, so I wasn't surprised. I don't know why the air conditioning didn't work, though.

Karl: Well, that wasn't the only thing that wasn't working properly. One of the machines in the gym was broken, too. But I suppose it was a very busy time, so the staff were probably just too busy to check it properly. These things happen, don't they? It didn't matter to me!

Jenny: Right . . .

Karl: So . . . what should we do for our next holiday then? We could go somewhere completely different.

Jenny: I'm not sure. I was hoping we could go to the coast again, but with all the work I've got at the moment, we'll have to wait and see.

Karl: Okay, then . . .

[Pause]

Now listen again.

[The recording is repeated]

[Pause]

That is the end of Part 4.

[Pause]

You now have six minutes to check and copy your answers onto the answer sheet.

Note: Teacher, stop the recording here and time six minutes. Remind students when there is **one** minute remaining

That is the end of the test.

Sample answer sheet

UNIVERSITY of CAMBRIDGE
ESOL Examinations

SAMPLE

Candidate Name
If not already printed, write name in CAPITALS and complete the Candidate No. grid (in pencil).

Candidate Signature

Examination Title

Centre

Supervisor:
If the candidate is ABSENT or has WITHDRAWN shade here

Centre No.

Candidate No.

Examination Details

PET Paper 1 Reading and Writing Candidate Answer Sheet 1

Instructions

Use a **PENCIL** (B or HB).

Rub out any answer you want to change with an eraser.

For **Reading:**
Mark ONE letter for each question.
For example, if you think **A** is the right answer to the question, mark your answer sheet like this:

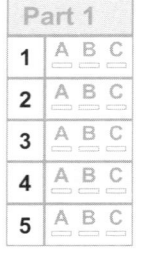

Part 1	Part 2	Part 3	Part 4	Part 5
1 A B C	6 A B C D E F G H	11 A B	21 A B C D	26 A B C D
2 A B C	7 A B C D E F G H	12 A B	22 A B C D	27 A B C D
3 A B C	8 A B C D E F G H	13 A B	23 A B C D	28 A B C D
4 A B C	9 A B C D E F G H	14 A B	24 A B C D	29 A B C D
5 A B C	10 A B C D E F G H	15 A B	25 A B C D	30 A B C D
		16 A B		31 A B C D
		17 A B		32 A B C D
		18 A B		33 A B C D
		19 A B		34 A B C D
		20 A B		35 A B C D

Continue on the other side of this sheet →

PET RW 1   DP491/389

© UCLES 2012   Photocopiable

Sample answer sheet: Paper 1 *Sample answer sheet*

SAMPLE

For Writing (Parts 1 and 2):

Write your answers clearly in the spaces provided.

Part 1: Write your answers below.

		Do not write here
1		1 1 0
2		1 2 0
3		1 3 0
4		1 4 0
5		1 5 0

Part 2 (Question 6): Write your answer below.

Put your answer to Writing Part 3 on Answer Sheet 2 →

Do not write below (Examiner use only)

0 1 2 3 4 5

© UCLES 2012   Photocopiable

167

UNIVERSITY OF CAMBRIDGE ESOL EXAMINATIONS 0090/1
English for Speakers of Other Languages
PRELIMINARY ENGLISH TEST

PAPER 1 Reading and Writing
ANSWER SHEET 2

Candidate Name

Centre Number

Candidate Number

Answer Sheet for Writing Part 3

S A M P L E

INSTRUCTIONS TO CANDIDATES

Write your name, Centre number and candidate number in the spaces above.

Write your answer to Writing Part 3 on the other side of this sheet.

You **must** write within the grey lines.

Use a pencil (B or HB).

Do **not** write on the barcodes.

© UCLES 2012 Photocopiable

Sample answer sheet: Paper 1 *Sample answer sheet*

You must write within the grey lines.

Answer only one of the two questions for Part 3.
Tick the box to show which question you have answered.
Write your answer below. Do not write on the barcodes.

Part 3	Question 7 ☐	Question 8 ☐

Examiner Mark:

© UCLES 2011

S A M P L E

Sample answer sheet

Sample answer sheet: Paper 2

UNIVERSITY of CAMBRIDGE
ESOL Examinations

SAMPLE

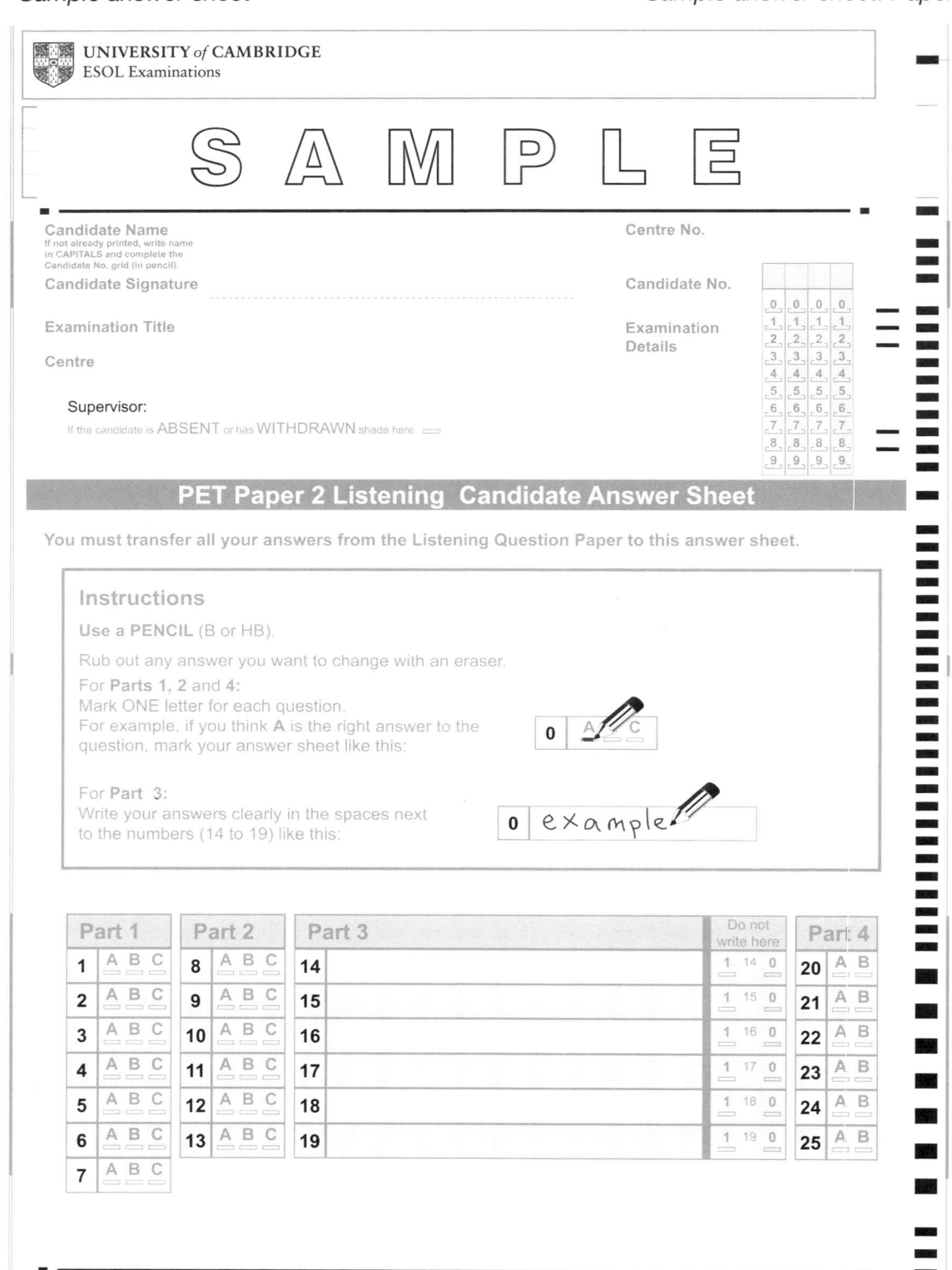

Candidate Name
If not already printed, write name in CAPITALS and complete the Candidate No. grid (in pencil).

Candidate Signature

Examination Title

Centre

Supervisor:
If the candidate is ABSENT or has WITHDRAWN shade here

Centre No.

Candidate No.

Examination Details

PET Paper 2 Listening Candidate Answer Sheet

You must transfer all your answers from the Listening Question Paper to this answer sheet.

Instructions

Use a **PENCIL** (B or HB).

Rub out any answer you want to change with an eraser.

For **Parts 1, 2** and **4**:
Mark ONE letter for each question.
For example, if you think **A** is the right answer to the question, mark your answer sheet like this:

For **Part 3**:
Write your answers clearly in the spaces next to the numbers (14 to 19) like this:

Part 1	Part 2	Part 3	Do not write here	Part 4
1 A B C	8 A B C	14	1 14 0	20 A B
2 A B C	9 A B C	15	1 15 0	21 A B
3 A B C	10 A B C	16	1 16 0	22 A B
4 A B C	11 A B C	17	1 17 0	23 A B
5 A B C	12 A B C	18	1 18 0	24 A B
6 A B C	13 A B C	19	1 19 0	25 A B
7 A B C				

PET L

DP493/391

© UCLES 2012 Photocopiable

Acknowledgements

The authors and publishers acknowledge the following sources of copyright material and are grateful for the permissions granted. While every effort has been made, it has not always been possible to identify the sources of all the material used, or to trace all copyright holders. If any omissions are brought to our notice, we will be happy to include the appropriate acknowledgements on reprinting.

Text on p. 40 adapted from *The English Review* (p. 17), November 2002, published by Phillip Allan, Hodder Education; text on p. 59 adapted from 'Gertrude, Benham, Mount Fay and Kaufmann Brothers'. Copyright © Dave Birrell, www.peakfinder.com. Reproduced with permission; text on p. 60 adapted from 'Francesco Da Mosto' by Aoife O'Riordain, *The Independent* 29.10.06. Copyright © The Independent 2006; text on p. 79 adapted from *Folktales and Legends of East Anglia* (pp. 26–28) by Geoffrey Dixon, 1996, published by Minimax Books Limited.

Colour section
Photo 1B: John Birdsall/Press Association Images; Photo 1C and 4C: Cambridge ESOL; Photo 2C: Photolibrary Group/All Canada Photos/Henry Georgi; Photo 3B: Photolibrary Group/Age Fotostock/Frank Siteman; Photo 4B: Photolibrary Group/Robert Harding Travel/Richard Cummins.

Black and white section
p. 16 (6): Shutterstock/Raisa Kanareva; p. 16 (7): Thinkstock/Medioimages/Photodisc; p. 16 (8): Shutterstock/Diego Cervo; p. 16 (9): Shutterstock/Alberto Zornetta; p. 16 (10): Veer/Rui Vale de Sousa; p. 19: Shutterstock/Mike Norton; p. 20: © David Wall / Alamy; p. 22: Stapleton Historical Collection/HIP/TopFoto; p. 36 (6): Shutterstock/qingqing; p. 36 (7 & 9), 56 (8) and 76 (9): Thinkstock; p. 36 (8): Shutterstock/Martin Allinger; p. 36 (10): Shutterstock/Aletia; p. 40: © 2005 TopFoto; p. 42: Shutterstock/OlegDoroshin; p. 56 (6 & 9) and 76 (6 & 7): Thinkstock/Jupiterimages; p. 56 (7): Shutterstock/ZouZou; p. 56 (10): Thinkstock/Siri Stafford; p. 59: Shutterstock/Lazar Mihai-Bogdan; p. 60: CAMERA PRESS/Karen Robinson; p. 76 (8): Shutterstock/Yuri Arcurs; p. 76 (10): Shutterstock/PT Images; p. 80: Shutterstock/Claudia Veja; p. 82: Shutterstock/Nataliya Hora.

Picture research by Diane Jones

Design concept by Peter Ducker MSTD

The CDs which accompany this book were recorded at dsound, London.